Just for Thought

ARTICLES OF MOTIVATION

MICHAEL E. PAYTON, MA

authorHOUSE®

AuthorHouse™
1663 Liberty Drive
Bloomington, IN 47403
www.authorhouse.com
Phone: 1 (800) 839-8640

Published by AuthorHouse 06/27/2018

ISBN: 978-1-5462-4874-3 (sc)
ISBN: 978-1-5462-4873-6 (e)

Library of Congress Control Number: 2018907612

Print information available on the last page.

DEDICATION

This book is dedicated to my wife Vicki. We have certainly been down a wild road over the years but have also two great sons, two great daughter-in-laws, three beautiful granddaughters and a whole bunch of memories!

Thanks for coming along for the ride. Let's keep it going for many more miles!!!!

Love, Mike!!

FOREWORD

During my professional career as a coach, teacher, administrator and public official one common issue I consistently dealt with was the need to motivate others and help them find ways to grow.

Whether it be a group of young men playing little league for the first time helping them develop enough self-confidence to "believe" they can hit the ball, working with a group of special needs students to develop self-esteem and personal growth despite the many obstacles they face, a human resources counselor dealing with the self-assurance needs many employees require to consistently perform at a higher level or working with small communities to believe they too are as good and as important as any community anywhere, the need for self-assurance, high self-esteem and increased personal growth are all elements needed for success.

I have never made any secret that the principles I try to communicate to others, the principles I try to live by, and the principles I try to instill in my children have been developed by the observation of many other people I have met over the years as well as prayer and the belief that I am not someone who ever thought he had "all the answers." My parents always taught me and my brother Jerry that no matter how much we thought we knew we never know as much as we think we do! My point is that most of the principles discussed in the articles of this book are based on what people I have come to respect and work with have instilled in me over the years.

I am very proud of the relationships I have developed, not just with "well-known" people but others who work day to day, raise their families, and are essentially what the Great American Dream is all about. Their motivation is the love for their families and their drive is a great work-ethic and the desire to grow knowing that by growing themselves, those they care about most would grow as well.

There will always be a debate as to whether success is synonymous with financial security. While there is plenty of fuel for both sides of that discussion, I do firmly believe that success is synonymous with great self-esteem, high value for both yourself and other people, and a sense of fairness and the ability to be open-minded but not easily swayed in your beliefs and principles that have been developed over a period of years.

My hope as you read this book is you find at least one of the articles to stimulate you, help you find a void in your life, or maybe just cause you to evaluate where your life is and whether or not you are happy with where you are today.

CONTENTS

Article 1   Do You Have A Leadership Personality? 1
Article 2   Standing On Your Own Two Feet 4
Article 3   Hope: The Most Effective Of All Four Letter Words 7
Article 4   The Energy Of Hate 10
Article 5   Ambition 13
Article 6   Do You Know Your Limitations? 15
Article 7   How Do You Define Maturity? 17
Article 8   Commitment 19
Article 9   Is It Important That Your Success Match Others? 21
Article 10   How Do You Define Life? 24
Article 11   Are You A "Joiner"? 26
Article 12   Behaviors You Don't Need 28
Article 13   How Angry Do You Get? 30
Article 14   Do You Tell Yourself The Truth? 33
Article 15   Personal Boundaries 35
Article 16   Little Things That Cause Big Problems 38
Article 17   Identifying Your Core Values 40
Article 18   Developing A Plan To Move Forward 42
Article 19   The Importance Of Friends 44
Article 20   How Well Do You Deal With Guilt? 47
Article 21   The Value Of Friendship 50
Article 22   Fulfillment Of Life 52
Article 23   Leading Yourself As Well As Others 54
Article 24   Selling Yourself To Yourself 56
Article 25   Total Quality Life Management 58
Article 26   Negotiating With Yourself 61
Article 27   Fresh Thinking Leads To Fresh Attitude 63

Article 28   Communications Critical To Successful Development.... 65

Article 29   Creating Your Personal Development Plan...................... 68

Article 30   How We Cope With Worry Determines How We
              Cope With Life... 71

Article 31   Are You Growing Toward Your Vision?............................74

Article 32   The Gift Of Leadership... 76

Article 33   Overcoming Obstacles To Success 78

Article 34   Addiction, Recovery, Freedom, Faith 80

Article 35   Believing Is Necessary To Achieve 82

Article 36   Reaching Success And Fulfillment.................................. 84

Article 37   Standing For The Truth Is Never To Be Ashamed Of..... 87

Article 38   There Is Always Time To Quit Later................................ 89

Article 39   Leadership Is A Full-Time Role....................................... 91

Article 40   The Difficulty Of Staying On Track In Adversity 94

Article 41   What Is Your Significance? 96

Article 42   Men's Groups... 99

Article 43   Building Your Support System 101

Article 44   Better To Work Together 103

Article 45   What Does Marriage Really Mean? 105

Article 46   Choosing A Role Model... 108

Article 47   Keys to Success: Honesty & Trust 111

Article 48   Evaluating Our Values..114

Article 49   The Practice Of "Labeling" 118

Article 50   The Inner Circle... 120

Article 51   Do You Take Chances? 122

Article 52   Does Fear Control You?... 125

Article 53   Cooperation.. 128

Article 54   How Well Do You Listen?..131

Article 55   Coping With Failure... 134

Article 56   Keep On Moving... 137

Article 57   What Questions Should You Ask Yourself?................... 140

Article 58   Strategies For Coping.. 143

ARTICLE 1

DO YOU HAVE A LEADERSHIP PERSONALITY?

The term "leadership" usually comes up in conversations about business and corporate governance. But leadership also applies to our personal lives as well.

As parents shouldn't we be looked upon as leaders of our families? And shouldn't we display those characteristics which give our families the confidence to follow us in how they conduct their lives?

Many of us have heard the statement, "it takes a man to father a child but not every man is a father." The same scenario applies in the business world, i.e. "any person can be given a leadership position but that person may not be a leader."

As both a parent and having had several leadership positions over the years I have found that the same basic principles that apply to being a leader with family also apply to being a leader in the business world.

There are many characteristics that can be put on the table for discussion as to what makes a good leader both in the family setting and in the workplace. I would like to focus on four general areas that I believe common to both.

To begin, I think no matter who you are trying to lead, if you are not honest and open you are going to be doomed for eventual failure. People know when they are being lied to. Some of us take a little longer to realize it but sooner or later we all can figure out what is true and what isn't.

The old adage, "you are only told what you need to know," has been proven to be wrong time and time again. When people are not told the truth or when they have not been given the whole picture, there is a feeling of distrust and suspicion toward leaders. Once this mode exists, it is practically impossible to change.

Let me point out that we all have been in situations where some things just can't be discussed with everyone due to legal issues or safety issues. But most family members and employees have no problem accepting that providing there is not a history of proven lies and deceptions by the leadership. Most of us can accept the fact there are times we just can't be told everything but we have a difficult time accepting the fact that we can't be told anything anytime.

Leaders who can command the respect of their employees or their family members by being both honest and open as often as possible on as many issues as possible, do not have the problem of being looked at under a suspicious eye every time they make a decision or give instruction. These people have a history of being as honest and open as possible. Others know this and realize they may not being told everything that is going on but there is good reason for it and they eventually will know.

Being able to make a decision is a key personality trait for a good leader. It is obvious that anyone can make a decision; the question is how well thought out and researched is the decision. Good leaders, again on personal and business issues, rarely jump to a decision without looking at all options.

This does not mean that a good leader makes snap decisions based on the most popular option or least expensive or time consuming. Many times those are the absolute worst possible reasons to make any decision but the reality is those type of decisions have led to families not speaking, employees loosing jobs, companies closing and even wars being fought.

Sincerity is key for anyone who is leading. One of the biggest reasons we admired and followed our parents was because we knew they cared. They were sincere and conscientious. We never doubted what they wanted was good for all of us. The sincerity showed. Employees see the same thing in a good leader. Employees know when their employers care. Its evident in the fairness displayed, the compassion and in the quality of the product or service.

To be an effective leader you must develop certain personality traits. Some you may very well be born with and just have to improve on. Being comfortable in your life style, having high self-esteem, being able to positively interact with others and accept constructive criticism are all characteristics of a self-actualized person and in turn a great potential leader.

As I always tell my students, being a boss is saying "I." Being a leader is saying "we." Leadership is running a team all striving for the same goal for the same reasons. Being a boss is you striving for a goal for the love of power and control. Bosses are doomed for failure, both personally and professionally. Leaders are destined for success both personally and professionally.

ARTICLE 2

STANDING ON YOUR OWN TWO FEET

One thing I have found out over the years, if nothing else, is that children and grandchildren make you think about a lot of things.

Most of us as we grow up really never think too much about tomorrow, for we are always thinking about today. When we are young one of the most boring conversations we have is with older people telling us how to prepare to be old. Retirements, pension plans, planning for college, all nothing most young people want to hear a lot about. At least I didn't.

Now that I have reached the "golden years," as my kids say about me, I have come to understand why my parents were as concerned about my future as they were.

Parents want their kids to eventually be able to stand on their own two feet. In other words, parents want their kids to eventually be able to take care of themselves, to live their own lives, make their own decisions, and of course to be happy.

I have to admit that I hated the day each one of my kids moved out and to be honest I would still love having them at home. But there is a desire among all of us to want to spread our own wings. The issue for parents is to be sure the kids don't immediately fly into a wall.

So how do parents prepare their children to stand on their own two feet? And here's another question: are we standing on our own two feet?

Are we as adults still depending on our parents (if they are still living), or depending on others to make sure we meet our personal and financial obligations. Do we constantly borrow money rather than budget our paychecks? Do we make sure our families know where their next meal is coming from? Do we blame everyone else every time something goes wrong or do we admit our mistakes, try to correct them and move forward?

I think as parents we need to work at developing some "traits" in our children that will cause them to be responsible. We need to help our kids realize that being responsible includes not just "getting a job," but also planning for a future.

I am not just talking about a financial future but also a future that will give them the opportunity for happiness and self-fulfillment. Values and appreciation for the opinions of others need to be implemented into our children at an early age.

Really what I am saying is there are two parts too standing on our own two feet. Part one is what I call the personal part. We should be respectful of others and be responsible for our actions. Choosing our friends because of the people they are, not because of whom their families are or what type on money they may have.

Part two is the work part. Choosing professional goals that lead to financial stability and developing the discipline to move toward those goals regardless of the challenges that come along the way.

Maturity comes into play as we try to stand on our own two feet. And with maturity comes the ability to sacrifice. A person not willing to sacrifice anything is a selfish and unsuccessful person. And frankly a person who cannot compromise or even understand why other people have different thoughts and ideas is a person who is afraid of being challenged, afraid of criticism, and an individual who cannot adopt to the changing ways of life, hence not able to stand on their own. Time and life will pass them by because of their inability to move forward and stand on their own two feet. Some people call this living in a "bubble."

For our children and grandchildren, we want them to eventually be able to be successful both professionally and within themselves. We want them to be able to make their own decisions, work out their own problems, and understand and respect the opinions and thoughts of others. We want them to choose a profession that they are happy with, marry someone they love, raise their children with values and principles and above all, have care and concern for others.

Being able to stand on our own two feet is really a life-long process. The challenges, both professionally and personally, are sometimes almost unbearable. But the ability to cope, continually move forward regardless of the sacrifice, and maintain our moral and ethical beliefs is key to standing on our own two feet and is the ultimate goal we have for our children.

ARTICLE 3

HOPE: THE MOST EFFECTIVE OF ALL FOUR LETTER WORDS

When we mention the word, "hope," there are always a lot of different definitions that pop into our minds. In our current society "hope" is a word that is tossed around loosely and really not always accurately.

If you look back through history there are many examples of how this one little four letter word has been able to keep our entire civilization moving forward.

Stepping back in time to the earliest part of our nation's history, the Revolutionary War, I think it is fair to say that "hope" is the key element that kept soldiers fighting through those brutal winters with little food, medicine or ammunition. It was the hope of a new world, a new chance at a life free from a monarchy.

Then there was the hope shared by those men who sat down and developed the U.S. Constitution. This was a group of dedicated individuals who shared a great hope that the work they were doing would serve as the guideline and blueprint for our nation's future.

During World War II, the world shared the hope that this horrible and devastating attempt to take over mankind would be squashed and never raises its head again.

As we move forward "hope" became the weapon of choice for all of us who felt lost and turned away from during the Vietnam, Watergate, and 9-1-1 periods.

But then there are also the times when hope becomes the one thing we hold on to during personal and family crisis. We hold on to hope when we see our families devastated through the loss of a loved one or a horrible house fire, car accident or illness. It is the hope that things will get better and things will improve that lets us keep our sanity and maintain our responsibilities.

And it is hope that a parent or spouse has when the ravages of drug addiction, child abuse, or criminal action take control of a family member and helplessness and anger try to take over our rational thinking and actions.

As we all move through life with all of its ups and downs, we each have our different ways of coping. And we all know that life deals each one of us a "hand" and that "hand" is the one we have to play out. For some of us it's certainly not so good, for others, it sure seems like a better game. But when we fail to accept the challenges that lay before us in life, when we accept the fact that we can't improve our "hand," then the real problem begins. Hope gives us the opportunity to improve our hand. Hope gives us the ability to make "bad things good."

A couple of years ago we visited the St. Jude's Research Center in Memphis. Hope is so strong and powerful there among those young children. The Shiner's Hospital in Cincinnati and those other children's research centers around the country are so motivated by the power of hope.

So what is "hope"? Hope is the stimulant that keeps people going in the absolute worst and most desperate of times. This "thing," that has been around since the beginning of time.

Many can obviously relate "hope," in terms of religious belief. From a clinical point, it could in part be defined in part as determination, will power or "grit."

What I do believe is very obvious is that "hope" is a key force in our attempts to live a positive and productive life. Hope is a vital weapon we can all use in our fight against negativity, helplessness and despair. It is a weapon that has a long-proven record of success.

When our kids are born don't we have a hope that they will grow up healthy, wealthy and wise? Why can't we generate those positive thoughts toward our own lives and attitudes? HOPE....possibly the most effective of all four letter words!

ARTICLE 4

THE ENERGY
OF HATE

We all seek to build up our energy levels. We try to eat energy foods, drink energy drinks, work-out and try to get the required amounts of sleep and rest. We do all this for good health and high energy levels.

But sometimes I think we forget how to generate all of this energy in the proper areas. The question we should be asking ourselves is do we channel our energy levels in positive and productive directions?

One of the keys to self-fulfillment is achieving our desired goals and to do that we must direct our energy toward successful completion of those goals. And as we all know, many if not all achieved goals only come with periods of frustration.

So here is an interesting question, "Do we expend more energy on the negative rather than the positive?" Do we focus more intensely on bad than on good?

Frustration is the result of difficult if not what to appear to be impossible challenges. If you are working on a difficult problem on the job, spent many hours on it and still don't achieve the desired result, when you get home, don't you feel drained, wore out and just basically disgusted? You may lie down on the couch, drop off to sleep or just lay there replaying the whole day in your mind, getting more upset and intense again, and yes burning up even more energy.

What about when someone annoys you, causes you problems either personally or professionally? It could be marital problems, a teacher is constantly causing one of your children a problem at school, or bills continue to mount up and you feel helpless not being able to pay them either on time or at all?

Agitations, anger, hurt and hate start developing in our minds. We become frustrated, our blood pressure gets out of "whack," we find ourselves being "jumpy" and annoyed. Miserable could be a good description of our overall mood.

When these situations start occurring we find ourselves getting tired and just plain wore out. The energy level is low. It has been drained from our bodies. Hate and negative feelings in general burn our energy faster than positive feelings and positive outlooks.

When we hate, we normally hate for long periods of time. As the hate gets stronger or as it continues to exist, it just pours the energy levels from our bodies. We cannot stop the negativity within our minds. It wears on us, it starts occupying our every thought. We develop negative attitudes toward work, family and friends.

Hate feeds on misery and discontent. It feeds on negative situations and changes our entire personality.

If we allow hate and negativity to take over our bodies, we can drink all the energy drinks we want, eat all the health foods we want, but we will still be worn out, tired and depressed.

It is so easy to let hate build in our minds. It is a complete rush of energy all channeled in negative ways. And as our level of hate and misery increases, so does the amounts of energy being zapped from our bodies.

In order to have a successful and productive life we must learn to channel our energies toward the positive, dwell on our successes, look forward to new challenges and look at ways to overcome difficult situations rather than submit to them and their consequences.

Do not let hate extinguish your energy and drive. Work hard to recognize that in any challenge, indeed in any day, we are going to be faced with some difficulty, come into contact with someone who causes us problems or face unique situations. But as you recognize also be determined not to let frustration and disgust take over for mature and positive thinking designed to face and defeat that challenge.

Utilize your energy levels for positive productive results. Do not let hate destroy your success and happiness.

ARTICLE 5

AMBITION

Ambition has been debated over the years as to whether it is a good or bad thing. There have been essays, books and even movies about ambition.

I like to look at ambition like we look at a lot of other things in society. Ambition can be a good or bad thing depending on how it is approached.

We raise our children to prepare for their future. We encourage them to be successful, looking at not only a career they will be happy with but also a career that will be financially sound.

The biggest problem with ambition is it can become extremely ruthless if not channeled in the proper way. Somehow over the years ambition has become known in many circles as "having your own agenda," "stepping on others," and "selling out."

In many ways, ambition and corruption have come very close to being synonymous with each other. There is no doubt a lot of this feeling comes from arrests of various public figures, political and judicial. Bribing, extortion, and conspiracy have all been associated with people who try to climb the corporate or political latter and have been brought down one way or another.

I have come to believe that as we teach young people how to succeed in life, we need to teach them the importance of values, morals and consequences not just in their life decisions but in their professional decisions as well.

Somehow over the years more and more people want to take the "easy" road to success. They want to step over as many obstacles as they can regardless of the consequences that may result. The end product is more important than the building process. As most of us know, the reality is, there is no "easy" road to success but rather "short-cuts" that usually leave vital consequences to eventually be dealt with.

Ambition is a critical tool in success. There is absolutely no denying that motivation leads to ambition. The more motivated a person is the more likely he or she will strive to be successful in their selected goals. Where we seem to lack in our motivational techniques many times is in the emphasis of putting values and morals into the encouraging of ambition.

Maybe the more important point we need to examine is putting our values and morals into this process of teaching our young to succeed. Obviously as more and more "white collar" crime continues to rise and the news media continues to bring us more and more stories of people being arrested and sentenced for crimes associated with corruption or dare we say, greed, that these critical elements of the teaching process for success have either been totally left out or certainly not emphasized.

The teaching of ambition and encouraging others to become motivated and ambitious is a necessary task. The teaching of this with emphasis on fairness, integrity and compassion make it an admirable and responsible task.

ARTICLE 6

DO YOU KNOW YOUR LIMITATIONS?

We all quickly know in life what our limitations are. Or do we only assume we know what are limitations are?

If we really stop and think about it, the real question might involve whether we actually have limitations or if we succumb to the challenges that present a possible limitation on a skill, purchase or even relationship.

Buying a house is for many the first time a major limitation seems to hit us in the face. We go about looking for a nice home, wanting a certain amount of rooms, nice yard, maybe a double garage, and then, we see the price. We usually make an offer, and even if it is accepted, then followed by the bank approval. That's when many times we are told no. We are limited on how much we can finance.

The same above scenario can be used for buying a car or making any huge purchase. But for most of us, after the initial bruised ego, we generally look for a less expensive house or car and move on. Sometimes with purchasing power, our limitations leave us less room for creative financing or manipulation to get the product we want. We learn to settle for the best alternative.

It goes without saying many people also have physical limitations due to health issues, accidents or birth and the courage these people display in achieving goals and having a productive life are an inspiration.

With life we do have more "wiggle" room in adjusting our limitations if we choose to. And the desire or lack of desire to increase our limitations or boundaries is mostly up to us.

Many times we feel limited in life based on social issues. How many people do you know believe they have to follow in their parents footsteps because that's what is expected of them and nothing more. These people place limitations upon themselves.

Just because you grow up in a small town does not limit you from going to a major university. Granted the challenge may be greater than for someone who lives in the big city the university is in, but if there is a limitation, based on distance, it is really only because the student has put it on him or her self.

Relationships are very similar for many people in the area of limitation. I firmly believe one of the major reasons divorce rates are so high in this country is because many young people, particularly in small and rural areas, believe they are limited in who they date and marry. So they end up in an unhappy and unhealthy marriage. Again, limitations placed on themselves by themselves.

Limitations many times cannot be eliminated but they can be pushed. We should strive to look for alternatives to achieving goals, both personally and professionally. The initial limits we seem to have we should examine closely and determine to what extent we are actually contributing to the limitation.

Conquering limitations requires initiative, desire and courage. But to submit to what appear to be limitations on your happiness and lively hood without even a challenge results in low self-esteem, low confidence and a generally miserable life.

ARTICLE 7

HOW DO YOU
DEFINE MATURITY?

I remember one night watching Johnny Carson's show and John Wayne was the guest. Now if you know anything about John Wayne you know what a great and proud patriot he was.

This particular night was shortly before 18-year olds were given the right to vote. Wayne was setting on the couch when Carson brought out another young entertainer who I honestly don't recall was. The discussion got into the debate over 18-year olds voting. This young man said he was happy to see this happening and Wayne, sitting there silently, suddenly said, "Why?" The audience kind of gasped. Wayne then explained about the idea that someone getting to a certain age shouldn't be the only requirement to vote. Now what followed was a discussion about if 18 year olds can fight for their country why can't they have a say in choosing their country's leaders.

The whole point to this story isn't concerning whether 18 year olds vote or not but rather Wayne's point about maturity. And not just about voting.

Today legally in this country the age of maturity is 18. That doesn't necessarily mean you can do "anything" at 18 because there are still laws requiring the age 21. But for the sake of voting and several other issues, the age of 18 does the trick.

But is 18 mature? Let's go further, is 50 mature?

What really constitutes maturity and for that matter, how do we define maturity? Webster's defines maturity as, "fully developed as a person." If that is the case, then I think we can certainly agree there are a lot of folks over 18 that are not exactly fully developed. The age 18 may be mature in the physical sense, but certainly not always emotionally.

Did you ever hear the saying, "any man can father a child but not every man knows how to be a father?" The phrase applies to emotional maturity. The same can be said about driving a car. You may be able to get your driver's license at 16 but are you really ready to make some of the decisions required in driving situations not covered in driver's education class?

Maturity is not a set thing that once we hit a certain age just becomes part of us. Indeed maturity is an ever-growing process. For some of us that process moves faster than with others. Self-confidence and self-control are certainly key factors.

Who we associate with and how we choose our friends are also key factors in maturity. Dependability, accepting responsibility, respect of others and being respected by your peers are all factors that play into maturity.

So it's probably safe to say we all may need to work on our maturity process in one way or another. Do you throw temper tantrums? Do you want to fight at the drop of a hat? Do you spend your time listening to and spreading gossip? Do you think about your bills and responsibilities before you blow your pay check?

Maturity is part of being a totally self-actualized person. The age of emotional maturity varies with each of us. How we handle difficult situations is certainly a reflection of our maturity. We need to monitor ourselves periodically, determine where we are going and how productive we are. And make necessary adjustments. Age alone won't do it. We have to monitor our maturity levels just like we get on scales to measure our weight.

It seems like the Duke had a good point.

ARTICLE 8

COMMITMENT

Today I will be performing a marriage ceremony for a young couple. Most of us who have been married for any long period of time know there is a lot that goes into a marriage: love, understanding, bad times and good times. I suppose it could all be summed up in one word: commitment.

Commitment is really a big word. It takes in much more than marriage. Commitment is the key to a successful life.

When we start into school, our parents are committed to us having a good education. Probably not so much during the early years but as we get older we become committed to finishing high school, getting into college and getting a job. That is a basic commitment our parents and ourselves make during our adolescent period.

In a more general way as citizens we are committed to the success and prosperity of our communities and our country. This doesn't mean in order to be committed to your community you have to become a civic leader, serve on councils or be at the forefront of various public issues. You commit to your community when you pay your taxes, keep your grass cut; make sure your property is kept in good condition, safe and not an eyesore to neighbors. Indeed, being a good neighbor is a great commitment to your community.

We also commit to keeping our country strong and prosperous. We pay federal taxes for various national defense, infrastructure and for healthcare and retirement. We make a commitment that our country is and will stay the strongest and most respected in the world.

We also need to commit to ourselves. We need to commit to ourselves that as we go through life we will strive do develop and maintain values and morals that will not only help us move toward a successful life but will encourage our children, family and friends to follow. We need to commit to be a good person by example.

Committing to various goals is not easy just as committing to sharing your life with someone else is not easy. As human beings we are all different, we think differently, we all come from different backgrounds and cultures. The commitment to work together, not give in to temptations for short-cuts and to not abandon our principles and values will be our strongest weapons against adversity as we go through life.

Most likely if we can begin to teach our children early in life the value of commitment they will subconsciously develop that quality as they grow. We must teach by example, not walking away from our problems, but challenging them and defeating them. Teaching our children how to accept responsibility is instilling in our children the road to success, whether playing on a little league team or trying to be CEO of a major company, is filled with obstacles and the foundations they lay both with skills as well as values and moral fiber will the most effective tools they will ever have to achieve success.

IS IT IMPORTANT THAT YOUR SUCCESS MATCH OTHERS?

Sometimes I think many of us don't appreciate the success we have attained. There are a lot of reasons for this and I also think because we feel this way we underestimate ourselves and our accomplishments.

There is nothing wrong with looking at successful people's lives and careers and trying to model yourself after them. Actually reviewing successful people and their accomplishments is a fundamental tool in teaching personal development skills.

We have to be careful however that as we look at the success rate of others that we don't "diminish" those successes we have achieved.

Over the years I have worked with a lot of student athletes as well as students who strive to be athletes but never quite make it to the "super star" status they desire.

My point is that while some have athletic ability built into their genes, others have to work hard to be half as good. But when these students who have worked so hard to be half the ballplayer the "gifted" ones are, see them on the courts or fields they suddenly feel depressed and embarrassed. They forget the hard work and improvement they themselves have made to get where they are. Maybe they are not as great as the athletes but they have achieved tremendous success getting to a higher level than they once were.

Another example is grades. Again being a teacher I have had students who can literally complete their work within 20 minutes of getting the assignment. Other students struggle to not only complete the assignment but to get it correctly. They feel inferior to the "brains" but they don't realize the success they have achieved working to get where they are, even with a lower grade.

The same is true with employment. Most of us have jobs that are important and even vital in our communities and in society. They are not what you would call "high-profile," but they are jobs that require skill, intelligence and dedication. To do these jobs properly we must be successful. We should not feel worthless or unimportant due to the fact that they are not jobs that are discussed on the nightly news, six-figure jobs, or jobs that have huge benefit packages and get into the mind-set to believe we are not successful at what we do.

How often do we compare the success of the neighbor's children to our own? It is really easy to do but just because your son or daughter may not be a doctor or lawyer, is that a reason to think you were not successful because your children are in another profession, even though they are doing quite well for themselves and even raising your grandchildren. Do you believe because what appears to be a higher success level for your neighbor's children means you were not successful in raising your children?

Do you feel you are not successful in life because your house isn't as nice as the house next door or down the street? Does it bother you that your car isn't as new as some of the cars your friends drive. Do you feel less successful because of these things?

Although we all strive for success, we must keep our lives in perspective. Comparing success levels is like comparing apples to oranges in my book. We need to remember that success is individual in nature. Success breeds happiness. There is no question many things factor into success. To be self-actualized with high self-esteem and good values, confident in where your life has taken you and knowing the path you want your life to take are the key elements to success.

Admiring and respecting other people's success is a mature quality. Being blinded to our own accomplishments based on what others have achieved can only lead to depression, lack of self-confidence, and inferiority feelings which cause an unproductive life.

ARTICLE 10

HOW DO YOU
DEFINE LIFE?

It would be accurate to say if you asked a thousand different people how they defined their lives you would probably get a thousand different answers.

Do you remember hearing the saying, "you don't know how that guy feels till you walk in his shoes?" There is a lot of truth to that statement. We really don't know how another person feels about his or her life nor do we know the reasons. What may look great to us could actually be misery to the person you are looking at. If counseling has taught me nothing else over the years it has taught me that a package's contents can be deceiving by the way it is wrapped. Someone who is looking like a million dollars on the outside and appears to have the world going their way may easily be an internal time bomb ready to explode.

A lot of factors determine how we look at life. Age, sex, race, finances and environment are just a few that make up your definition of life.

Is it fair to say that if we want a true definition of what life is that we must know what we want out of life? Do we want a good marriage, children, a great job, no financial worries, religious fulfillment? Or do we want to travel, explore, never settle in one particular place or get involved in long-lasting relationships?

The truth is our lives are unique to each one of us. What is a very happy and fulfilling life to us may very well be a life of depression and chaos for another. There is no question environment plays a part in how we think about our lives. If you live in a poverty stricken area of the world your life is certainly defined differently than it would be if you lived in mid-town Manhattan.

There is no question that people who suffer long-term illness and disabilities would define life differently than someone healthy and full of energy might define it.

It would be a good drill to set down and make out a list of those things in your life that you are happy with and a list of those you are not. Once you make your lists you then have to weigh whether the good points out weigh the worst of the bad points. Are the bad points causing you depression, anxiety and economic distress? Next, ask yourself about the good things that make you happy? Are they keeping you happy, are they rewarding and do they occupy most of your conscious thoughts?

Chances are if you do this little drill and be honest with yourself, you will most likely find out not only how you define your life but what you need to work on to make it a better life.

Only we know how we define our lives. The key point is, are we happy with our definition of life? Happiness and a healthy life-style, both physically and emotionally, are great definitions of life to strive for.

ARTICLE 11

ARE YOU A "JOINER"?

Not to long ago I was talking with a friend about joining a civic club here in town. He was telling me about all of the various charity causes the club sponsors and the general sales pitch we've all got to join some club, organization or even church at one time or another.

I have been a member of several organizations ranging from the Masonic lodge, to Kiwanis, to the American Legion over the years. Throw into that mix a church, health club, and several other civic groups. I have met a lot of wonderful people and we have been able to do what I consider a lot of positive things for our area.

But in recent years all of the civic organizations and churches across the country report one common point: declining membership. Rarely do I attend any of these groups' meetings that the discussion of declining membership and nonpayment of dues doesn't come up. Also I might mention that many of these organizations have closed their doors in some communities. Most of the major civic groups report at least the loss of one or more of their community clubs each year across each state.

So why are some of the oldest and most established civic organizations in our country's history declining? Are these organizations no longer doing all the good things for their communities they once did? Are membership dues to high? Could it be that people are just too busy to join? What about the leadership in these groups? Is it effective?

Most likely all of the above reasons have some validity but you have to feel there is more to this story. Are people today more selfish of their time, their money and their concern for others?

It is hard to think that we have come to the place where we have lost concern for our fellow man. The question might relate to how we as people have evolved in our values and thinking over the years. Is community service a "big deal" in today's world or do we just not have time for it?

Have we actually become more selfish as people? Do we only want to be involved with that which is directly benefiting us as individuals?

Many "veterans" of these various organizations say that today's young people "just don't care." Others point out that today's young people want to come into a club, take over and do it their way. And if they can't do it their way, then it is the highway. So obviously traditional versus non-traditional is a factor to be considered.

I do believe many of our young people really do care about their fellow man. I think they have fresh, innovative and even controversial ways of getting their points across. How many times have you heard someone say, "That's the way we've always done it..?" But as a country look how we have grown over the years. Have there not been many fresh, innovative and controversial ideas that have helped shape our nation.

So my point is, could change or the fear of change, be a reason for memberships and volunteer organizations decreasing? I believe young people today do not mind joining groups and organizations. And many of the organizations they join are the progressive ones. Those that tend to stick with the past unfortunately die with the past. But young people want to join organizations where they can contribute too and see progress evolve. It's a different generation, it's a different time. Joining isn't really the issue. It might be the issue is letting go of the past.

ARTICLE 12

■────────────────────

BEHAVIORS YOU
DON'T NEED

There are certain behaviors that when present in our lives create barriers to our future success. These behaviors are sometimes initiated by our family members, our neighbors, co-workers, people we socialize with and our general environment. If we choose to move forward in life, it becomes necessary to eliminate these behaviors as they become stumbling blocks for a successful future.

I've always told my first year college students that one of the hardest adjustments they will make is eliminating people from their lives that seek to hold them back. Some will want to hold you back because of jealousy, not wanting to see someone get ahead if they can't either. Another reason is that some people just become satisfied with where they are in life and have no desire to move forward or encourage others around them to do so. As you move further in your education, you begin spending more time with other students, getting involved with the school environment, i.e. schedules, homework, special projects, etc., and you develop a new group of friends and associates which continually pulls you away from your previous lifestyle. Suddenly one day, you think, "hey, I haven't seen Johnny in a long time." Well, Johnny is fazing himself out of your life by not wanting to support or move forward with you.

Besides environmental behavior, there are several other behaviors that you really don't need in your life if you want to move forward. Some of these behaviors can actually suck the energy and initiative right out of your mind and body.

Negativity is, in my opinion, as rapidly contagious as the common cold but with many more far-reaching consequences. If you think about it for a moment, remember the last time you were around an individual who was complaining about something or someone: continual criticism or negativity. Not one positive comment. If you recall, you may very well have started agreeing, even though you are not really sure why. People with negative behaviors bombard everyone with rapid verbal venom at an almost incredible pace. Before you know it, you are absorbed into their web and start the same behavior.

Underestimating your own capabilities and lacking self confidence needed to achieve career or personal advancement is a fatal behavior for someone trying to move to a successful lifestyle. Developing self-confidence is critical to any success. Remember, if you have developed enough confidence to learn new skills, change your living environment and dare to dream of a brighter future, you have the strength needed to keep on going.

Do not succumb to bullying. Do not let other people push you in career or personal life directions you do not feel comfortable with. Getting off the desired track or direction you want to move toward is difficult enough without letting others try to head you in directions they feel are better for you or where they feel that one day may make you more valuable to them. Spouses forcing their mates into career directions not suited for them or friends talking friends into changing colleges or majors are examples of bullying through intimidation that can crush plans for future success.

We all have our freedom to choose what lifestyle we want to pursue. We also have the right to set up our own game plan to achieve that goal. Eliminating behaviors and habits from our current way of life and replacing them with those more conducive to the direction we want our lives to move is critical to success.

ARTICLE 13

HOW ANGRY DO YOU GET?

There isn't one of us who hasn't gotten angry or "mad" at one time or another. It's part of our human make-up. Anger is normal, just like being happy, or talking, laughing, crying, being hungry, etc. But anger, like the others must be controlled before reaching a certain point. If left uncontrolled many consequences can occur and several are bad.

Unlike other emotions, anger does seem do get us into more controversial situations, also known as "trouble." With other emotions we may get on other people's nerves, but we usually don't go the extremes, violence in particular, like we many times do when angry.

Psychologists and therapists like to go back into an individual's past, search their upbringing, how their parents treated them, and many other areas to find the "root" of an anger problem. There is nothing wrong with those techniques but unfortunately our anger many times must cause a problem before therapy is sought. And sometimes that therapy is initiated by the legal system which is the result of some bad situations our tempers have gotten us into.

Without getting into complex anger management techniques, I thought I would share what I call "Common Sense" techniques for controlling our anger. If we can control our tempers and emotions on an accepted level with society day to day, we will find our lives much more productive and enjoyable.

It is important to keep in mind that certain day to day events can cause our anger to raise, usually not to violent levels, but we can become increasingly irritable. For example, the simple hectic pace of getting up in the morning and getting ourselves and our kids off to work and school, heavy traffic, alarm clocks that don't go off, a boss that is in a bad mood.....the list goes on and on. The question is how far do we let these issues affect our daily lives? How far do we let small things affect our entire future?

First, take a time out before you say something you may regret later. All of us need to use the "time out" technique, not just children. Walk into another room, go outside, and if possible just find some way to get away from the situation for a few minutes. Don't get baited into saying something that will most likely end up hurting you more than it will ever hurt who you are talking to. A few short minutes away from a "situation" can literally save you years of regret.

Try to get some exercise after you feel the anger building up. Depending on where you are this isn't always easy but if at work, if possible go for a walk during lunch, if at home, take a walk, cut the grass, wash the car, even go to the local store and just walk around. Physical activity does wonders for stress. Many days I try to go to our local health club just to move around in a different environment for an hour or so; burning off the stress is as important as burning off the calories.

Look for alternatives. In some cases this is almost impossible but in many cases it works to perfection. If you are someone who has difficulty with being late for work because of heavy traffic, on a day off explore a few different routes to work. You may have to leave a little earlier, but you might be in a better mood when you get to work. Sometimes it may be that you just have to start getting up earlier and leaving earlier. If you have kids you have to get off to school, then get yourself up earlier, have an extra cup of coffee, take a morning jog or just go out and sit on the back porch for a few minutes before you get the kids out of bed. Your attitude as you start the day easily dictates how your day can go.

Finally, I would ask you to think before you speak. Words are worse than bullets. They can be daggers to the heart. What you say in a moment of rage may never be forgotten. Forgiven yes, but many times never forgotten. Many people have lost promotions on jobs because of something they may have said years ago in a moment of anger. Many children's' impressions of their angry and violent parents when angry never leave their minds. It is an invisible barrier that can't be removed. And marriages and friendships are ruined when one or both say things to each other in a moment of anger and rage.

These are just some basic "Common Sense" techniques I thought were worth mentioning to maybe help keep you from some embarrassing or even dramatic long-lasting consequences in your life. I do recommend if you begin to recognize you are getting on edge too frequently, flying off the handle, even getting into fights, then please see your pastor, physician or seek other professional help. There is absolutely nothing embarrassing or wrong with realizing and seeking professional help. Actually realizing you need the help is half the battle.

ARTICLE 14

DO YOU TELL YOURSELF THE TRUTH?

Do you find it easy to lie to yourself? It's an interesting question. I would say that for many of us, we not only find it easy to lie to ourselves but we probably do it several times a day.

People have an amazing ability to see things as they want to see them, not as they are really seeing them. Many of us look at things that are going badly and say to ourselves this really isn't bad but is getting better when the truth is not only is something going badly it is getting worse. We do this in relation to health issues, relationships and financial situations to name a few areas.

Take health issues such as weight control and exercise. How many times have you told yourself, "one more beer, one more donut, or one more hamburger." We tell ourselves this isn't going to hurt us, we will walk it off, work out harder at the gym tomorrow, etc. But our conscious really knows we want more because of our own desires or ego, knowing full well none of the extra food or drink is really healthy and knowing full well we aren't going to work out any harder if at all.

With regard to relationships how many people are miserable today because they won't admit to themselves they are not compatible? They have little in common and no desire to compromise with their companion. We strive to make ourselves think we are happy. We go to church together, take the kids to the various school functions together, even hold hands and smile anytime we are in public. We keep up the "image" but deep down we know we are miserable. Do we stay with people, marry people, have children with people, not because we really love them but because we don't want to admit we are in a bad situation and our "friends" may look at us as failures or not include us in the big social events.

Perhaps we lie to ourselves more about finances than any thing else. We all love to spend money. How many times do we get our pay check and head to the stores to buy items not for need but for want? We tell ourselves many times that we will hold off on the rent payment this month and pay two payments next month so we can buy something when we know there is a slim to no chance of making a double rent payment the next month. Some of us also buy cars, clothes, even houses, knowing full well they cannot be afforded but we put that thought in the back of our mind and sign on the dotted line!

It's fair to say that we don't like to tell ourselves the truth because we are not happy in our current reality. Reality does slip in on us however, usually at the worst possible moment. Are we not truthful with ourselves because of pride, selfishness, even ignorance?

Being confident in ourselves and what we have achieved are two weapons to use when we start to lie to ourselves. Good self-esteem, sound and purposeful goals aimed at producing a quality life and a realization that although we don't have everything we want, we are on the road to a better tomorrow for ourselves and our families are qualities which make lying to ourselves less appealing and really more insulting to us.

ARTICLE 15

PERSONAL BOUNDARIES

I like to compare personal boundaries to garden fences. Farmers put garden fences up to keep animals and other "critters" away from the corn, cabbage, carrots and other vegetables planted in the garden. We need to put up personal boundaries as a fence to protect ourselves and let people know when they are behaving in such a manner that it is unacceptable to our values, morals and life style in general.

A question we need to look at is, "Do you have a right to protect yourself emotionally as well as physically?" Very few people would argue that if an individual was being attacked by someone with a club, gun or just hit with a fist that they have the right to protect themselves and fight back. A person also has the right to avoid people who they believe may cause them physical harm. An individual who recognizes particular environments such as certain bars, dark alleys or even so-called "friends" homes, will lead to trouble would not be blamed for avoiding those areas.

It is vitally important to ourselves that we set personal boundaries as well as physical boundaries. In order to have a healthy personality we must develop the ability to speak up for ourselves. Failure to be able to define a set of personal boundaries that define your morals, values, principles, is a sure way to not live a self-actualized life. When you are unable to defend yourself emotionally as well as physically, you open the door to being controlled by others therefore not being in control of your own life.

Communication in setting personal boundaries and is a key to success. In no way am I saying that setting boundaries is easy. It requires courage, discipline and being honest with ourselves. Definitely you must be able to have honest communication with those around you but you must also have honest communication with yourself. If there are things or people in your life that causes you discomfort or stress, you must accept the reality that they will only go away if you decide you want them to go away. Sometimes this is extremely difficult. This process can require loss of friendships, loss of family relationships, loss of job or even loss of relationship with our own children.

There are many different techniques you can research relating to communication with self. These are techniques developed by professional psychologists, psychiatrists and counselors over a period of years with much trial and error. They are techniques that need to be related to you in a more clinical setting but keep in mind that realizing you may need to explore these techniques means you are indeed beginning to understand you are not happy with something or somebody in your life.

If we agree we should treat all human beings with dignity and respect then why shouldn't we also agree to treat ourselves with dignity and respect? Many people develop, through environment from birth or just poor choices in friends, feelings of not being worthy of respect, shame of inadequacy and feelings of always trying to be accepted. As this attitude is reinforced in them over their lifetime, the qualities of self-respect and independence fade away and are difficult if not impossible to rekindle.

Setting boundaries for what we will and will not accept emotionally, what we will not permit to violate our values, morals and lifestyle is a key to moving forward with our self-actualization and future success. Good support systems are a great asset in setting your boundaries. Placing yourself in environments where your principles and how you choose to live your life already exist are excellent starts in developing your "personal boundary" fence.

Remember, setting boundaries are not an attempt to control another person, although don't be surprised many people who are "control freaks" will try to convince you it is, setting boundaries is a crucial step in taking control of our own lives, of letting the only person who should be controlling our lives control it....yourself!

ARTICLE 16

LITTLE THINGS THAT
CAUSE BIG PROBLEMS

In relationships I think it is fair to say that is virtually impossible to find two human beings who share the same quirks, habits, and even likes or dislikes. It is how the compromises on those differences occur that determine whether a solid, long-lasting relationship can last.

Many marriage therapists and psychologists will tell you that when marriages collapse the primary reason is neither partner has the desire or maturity to compromise or at least understand the opposite partner's feelings and attitudes.

Our belief systems and values contribute to how we relate to other people. Many times, especially if the partner or the friendship is especially meaningful to us, we tend to take more than give. We tolerate small irritants because we value the relationship. The problems however begin to develop internally on our subconscious and over a period of time build up resentment, tension and sometimes violence.

Feeling controlled is considered in most studies to be one of the most common relationship complaints. How many times have you heard people say, "Nobody tells me what to do?" That attitude may sound independent and bold but it can eventually leave you with a lonely life and deep bitterness. Remember control can be looked at in two ways: (1) dominating or (2) over reaching concern for your welfare.

Dominating control people want to control because it's their personality. They have to be in charge. Make the rules. Call the shots. People who try to control with over reaching concern for your welfare, are well-intentioned, usually extremely loyal, and concerned about your well-being to a point of smothering you. One the one hand, you really can come to hate the dominate controller. One the other hand, you can actually run away from the over-reaching controller. You would rather die as hurt their feelings. So you continue to feel miserable but fear offending.

Be care in a relationship to criticize to quickly. Criticizing every little move weighs on anyone's nerves. Criticism on a regular basis, no matter how small, grows slowly but steadily. Eventually you make your partner feel inappropriate and even unloved. The little criticisms are suddenly huge boulders in the relationship causing separation. Be careful how you criticize and determine if the criticism is worth the possible outcome later on. Again, it can be something small that can grow to disaster.

The key to controlling the little problems before they become big fiascos is communication. The more communication couples have in relationships the better. Honesty about what bothers you, what you like and don't like, and being able to accept the other partner's viewpoint helps slow down years of continual built-up anxiety and hate.

Try hard to respect your partner's ideals and values. Don't ridicule or attack. But also be aware that communication is a two-way street. As you encourage your partner to communicate with you, it is your responsibility to communicate back as well. Holding little things inside can only be corrected if both partners are willing to communicate.

ARTICLE 17

IDENTIFYING YOUR CORE VALUES

Have you ever given thought to what your core values are? We all have certain basic beliefs or values that we tend to always let be our guide in everyday behavior.

But where do these core values come from? How did we develop and sustain them over our life time?

For many of us, core values come from our childhood. They are engrained in us via our parents and the community we were raised in. Good work ethic, politeness, respect for self and others, compassion and integrity. All of these are core values that we have grown up refining.

But core values can also be bad. If you are an individual who has been raised in an atmosphere of greed, selfish interests and lack of compassion or caring for your fellow man, although these are true core values, they are negative core values meaning they will prevent you from a more successful and meaningful life.

In determining your own core values, take a simple test. Ask yourself what you are interested in. What do you like to do in your spare time? What are the things that make you the happiest? Where do you feel most comfortable? What are the things you don't like to do? What places make you the most uncomfortable? Answering these questions to yourself truthfully will give you a good sense of where you values system is.

Core values primarily dictate how people understand the difference between right and wrong. If you are not sure what peoples core values are, the best way to find out is just watch them. How do they act and behave on a regular basis? And more importantly, observe how they act in times of crisis or emergency. How people act when the chips are down, when it is "crunch" time, reflect a person's core values more genuinely than any other test.

So can you change your values system? Can you manipulate your values system? Certainly you can. Obviously we want our values system to be one of respectability and integrity. As you evaluate your values, ask yourself some intense questions that only you can answer: Do you have a strong work ethic? Do you believe in God or attend church? Do you spend as much time as possible with your family? Are you disgusted with lying, cheating and stealing? Your honest answers to those questions will tell you much about yourself.

Remember, your core values are your fundamental beliefs. They are what guide your behavior, attitude, indeed your very personality. If you aren't happy with how your life is going, it may be time to go back to basics: evaluate your core values.

ARTICLE 18

DEVELOPING A PLAN
TO MOVE FORWARD

Everyone needs to know where they are going in life. Many people will tell you they wanted to be a teacher, doctor or lawyer when they grow up, and a lot of those people achieved these goals. But there are many of us who really don't know where we want to go, even after we have finished high school and paid thousands of dollars for some degree. Its like, "OK, I graduated, now what?"

In order to move forward with our lives we need to develop a plan of direction. We must evaluate where we are now and if we are not happy, we need to look for a new direction.

There are several areas for consideration as you develop a plan of action to move forward with your life. To begin, you need to have a vision for yourself. Where do you see yourself if you want to move in another direction? Do you see yourself in management, owning your own business or possibly working for a major company? Have a vision for yourself, an ultimate and achievable goal.

You need to think about where you are physically. Age, health, family concerns. It is important you evaluate your life as it currently is. Ask yourself how much time you want to allow reaching your vision. Older people may want to move forward in a manner that will accomplish what they want but at a different pace. Younger folks, may because of children or other financial obligations not want to spend a lot of time working toward a vision that will take months or years to achieve because of the time restraints placed on them by their children and families.

Try to set high standards for yourself. Don't try to skate by but set standards and requirements that are both difficult to achieve but worth the effort. Remember the investment you make in preparing yourself for the vision you want to achieve is also an investment in your family as well.

Do not be afraid to make hard decisions. A strong vision with a profitable result is only going to happen if sacrifice occurs. Do not "slack" on making decisions just because they are hard. Time away from family and friends, living on tight budgets, and even difficult work hours are hard decisions you may have to make to achieve the ultimate goal. If the vision you have set is worth it to you, then you must make those hard decisions that will eventually lead to its fruition.

Do not be ashamed to plan for and work toward the future. Living for today is just that. Many people live pay check to pay check. Some go through each month wondering if their electric or water will be turned off. They even wonder if they can feed their children each day. As you plan and work toward a productive future, be proud of the vision you have set. Be proud of the goals you have already achieved leading toward the vision you see for yourself. Don't ever apologize for working to make your future and your family's future better.

Finally, never ever give up. There are going to be road blocks, some tougher than others. Cooperation with family and friends will not always be what you want. But keep your vision in mind. Live by the high standards you have set for yourself. Don't be afraid to make hard decisions when those times come. And never apologize or be ashamed of trying to make a better life.

ARTICLE 19

THE IMPORTANCE OF FRIENDS

When the discussion of friends and why we have them comes up, there are a variety of reasons but the reality is having friends gives us a feeling of purpose. We all want to have at least one person who likes us, confides in us, gives us advice and even fights with us. And we want to have at least one person we can return the same favors too.

Our Friends shape who we are. Friends keep us psychologically sound in the most intense and traumatic times of our lives. Our relationships are a direct result of some type of friendship. Who we work with, who we party with, even who we marry, are many times directly or indirectly related to friendships of some sort.

Friendships start at the very early stages of life. It is common to hear children talk about their "best friend." There is usually a common bond of sorts that brings children together during their early years. Sometimes the bond increases as they get older and even extends into adulthood.

Many times we tend to form our priorities based on friendships. We have a tendency to pick friends who are similar to us. The saying, "likes attract likes," is true. This can be good but can also be just the opposite. For example, if you are an individual who is very laid back, maybe unorganized and "fly by the seat of your pants," you may choose friends with those same characteristics. This can sometimes cause future problems if someone has never been exposed to the more formal, organized and well structured lifestyle of others. People need to experience "how the other half" lives.

Here is one additional example. As a former school teacher I have been able to show that when you group a child with average grades with a group with above average grades, the child's grades do improve. Friendships are formed with the group, study habits improved and social interaction making the child feel happier and with more self-worth occur. Because of the friendships the student's life has become more rewarding.

An interesting comment on friends involves friendships of separate genders. While most early friendships are with the same sex, as we get older we start branching out more. School activities, social activities and a variety of other reasons open the doors for friendships of the opposite sex. The friendships don't always end up romantic. Actually many times when a long-term friendship turns into a serious romantic situation, the entire relationship falls apart. Studies have shown that most successful romantic relationships are not the result of long-term friendships. Sometimes your spouse becomes your best friend, but that's usually not the way the relationship began.

Many men have legitimate friendships with women and visa versa. It is not uncommon today to have married men or women who confide more in another married person of the opposite sex. Lots of insecurities do develop in marriages because of spousal friendships with the opposite sex but keep in mind; these friendships are not discreet or clandestine. Many spouses know who their mate's close friends are. Friendship and a romantic relationship do not have to be synonymous.

Be careful in developing on-line friendships. Some people tend to be more open and uninhibited with on-line relationships. Deception is a product of on-line relationships at times. People "spill their guts" more easily when they are at a keyboard. They begin to build a trust, that although many times genuine, there are many times it is a path to problems. People have sent money to on-line friends, given out their social security number, credit card and bank account numbers believing they are helping a friend. The results have been devastating. Being taken advantage of by on-line friends has sadly become to much the norm in our society.

It's fair to say we want friends because we don't want to go through life lonely. There is absolutely nothing wrong with that reason. Friends make us feel good about ourselves, they improve our self-worth; build up our confidence and most of the time makes us more productive as a person. Choose your friends wisely based on caring, respect and trust. True friendships are invaluable.

■ ───────────────

HOW WELL DO YOU DEAL WITH GUILT?

There are a variety of factors that determine how we deal with guilt. And interestingly enough, what is guilt for one individual may be nothing at all to someone else.

It isn't fair to really assume that our upbringing is the only factor that determines the guilt feelings we may experience. There are many people raised in very strict religious backgrounds, some in agnostic backgrounds and some who although professed to some religious affiliation, all may experience similar forms of guilt feelings at one time or another but also may very well have extremely different parameters of guilt feelings for similar incidents.

Overall we can say that guilt is a feeling or emotion that occur when we believe we have done something wrong or something that has caused some type of uncomfortable problem or issue for someone else. We begin to examine that particular behavior to see what we can do to make sure it does not occur again.

Guilt doesn't always relate to hurting someone's feelings. We can experience guilt feeling for eating more than we should, drinking more, or not spending enough time with our friends or family.

Weight control and exercise seem to come with built-in guilt factors. Most of us worry about weight at one time or another. We feel guilty when we have an extra candy bar or Big Mac. Not that we don't go ahead and eat them, we just know that the reality is we are hurting ourselves.

Being away from family and friends, many times because of work schedules, is a common guilt complex many people have. Missing your children's ballgames, school plays and other family events because of your employment has led many people to either change jobs or just flat out quit working. Some of those options obviously lead to other problems but the guilt issue becomes so intense it seems the only resolution.

In the broad sense, guilt is usually situational. If we do something bad, either intentionally or unintentionally, that hurts someone physically or emotionally, we do feel bad and want to be sure we don't do it again. Apologizing usually makes us feel better immediately but the realization we hurt someone and don't want to do it again is the key to changing the behavior.

Changing the behavior from unacceptable to acceptable is the key to learning from guilt. Sometimes the behavior can be changed faster than at other times. Much of it is the situation the particular action occurred. Some situations can be rectified easier than others. With diet, for sure you can cut down on eating frequently quicker than you may be able to change your work schedule. But you at least realize the behavior causing the guilt.

Here is another point to make regarding guilt. You must admit to yourself you cannot change the past. Continuing to beat yourself over the head is only punishing yourself and those around you. Accepting the fact you acted inappropriately, doing everything you can do to make amends with those affected, and making sure you have changed your behavior so as to not repeat what has occurred, is all you are expected to do in most cases. Moving forward with your life is the next step. You must be able to move forward and not let the "guilt trip" ruin the rest of your life. Obviously in some cases there may be extenuating circumstances that require consequences. If you have broken a law you may very well spend some time either on probation or possibly in jail, but even in those cases, recognizing what you did and changing your behavior to never do it again is a step forward.

Guilt needs to be looked at as a tool that teaches us to either modify or eliminate a particular behavior. Use it in a productive manner to lead you to a more self-actualized life.

ARTICLE 21

THE VALUE OF FRIENDSHIP

Friendships vary in scope. We have all heard of childhood friendships, best friends, BFF's and all the other labels that go with what is generally referred to as friendship.

As children, we see our friends almost every day. School, youth sports, church and many other neighborhood activities make it easy to see those we call our friends on a regular basis. We confide in each other, tell each other "secrets" and even argue and fight with each other from time to time. But the bonds that hold us together, meaning our life situations at the time, allows us to let bygones be bygones and forgive and forget.

When we move out of the adolescence stage and into adulthood what we discover is that many of the childhood friends fade from our life because much of the common bonds that held us together are dissolved. Although those early childhood reasons for having friends were essential at that time, we find that a new approach to making and keeping friends is slowly developing in our lives. Now for sure some childhood friends do stay around, maybe throughout our lives, but most slip away as the reasons for those friendships not only become less important but totally vanish.

If you think about it, how many people who still may physically live close to you and were friends you once confided everything in, really now even in your weekly loop? Do you even see them just mowing the grass or pulling the car out of the driveway? Adulthood has a way of quickly and dramatically changing lives and friendships.

The question becomes what type of friends are we looking for as adults? Do we want friends that will advance our careers, give us a higher social status, or are we still looking for one or two people that we can totally confide in and they confide in us?

Once becoming an adult, I believe stability in a friendship is the key to maintaining and improving upon it. Stability in any relationship is hard for sure. Age, children, marriage and employment all are variables that cause a friendship to destabilize, sometimes in a very unhealthy manner.

As we become older with more family and personal responsibilities we also find we don't necessarily see even our "best" friends on a daily basis; maybe not even a monthly or annual basis. We may talk on the phone, text or use email, but the bond is still there, the friendship just as intact, but the physical presence not always.

Friendships do not have to be one hundred percent reciprocal. The fact is there are some partners in a friendship that do give more while other partners take more. It's the reasoning this occurs and the overall feeling of caring that bonds theses type of friendships. Equal reciprocation is not a requirement for a successful adulthood friendship.

Finally it is important to point out that as we age some friendships simply end because a partner passes or becomes too ill or unable to maintain the relationship. Stability of a friendship starts weakening more as the communication between the friends slows down or even ends.

Overall friendships, stable and maturing friendships, are critical to emotional growth and an opportunity for a self-fulfilled life. Nurture the friendships you have but realize that the relationship should not be considered a crutch that is needed for you to have a productive life.

ARTICLE 22

FULFILLMENT OF LIFE

When asked whether you feel fulfillment in your life, what would you answer?

It's an accurate assumption that many of us would never say we have a fulfilled lifestyle. Many of us always want something more, never satisfied with what we have and always looking for the "pot of gold" at the end of the rainbow.

People become fulfilled in life in many ways. For some people, it's all about career, money and status. Since the early school days boys want to grow up to be doctors and girls want to grow up to be nurses. Many of the first essays our teachers assigned had the heading, "What Do I Want to Do When I Grow Up."

Keep in mind there is absolutely nothing wrong with wanting a successful career and all that goes with it. The question is how much we let that desire control our lives. Do we become so obsessed with pursuing that goal we don't enjoy or appreciate the other things life has to offer along the way?

Fulfillment takes other forms for people rather than career. Many of us have a strong need to a spiritual commitment for our lives to be completely fulfilled. A relationship with God or a spiritual lifestyle not necessarily with Christianity is, for many people, the only way they will consider themselves fulfilled. Inner peace, faith and love are what many require while social status and material possessions don't figure into the equation.

A solid family structure is also a sign for other people that they have a fulfilled life. Being able to provide a safe home, put food on the table for the children and making sure they attend school, get a good education and marry moving forward with their own lives, with a secure job and children of their own, is how many of us determine whether we have achieved a fulfilled life.

There are various ways we all determine whether or not our lives have fulfillment or whether we are still struggling to achieve that goal, but there are a few things that we all should have in common as we search for fulfillment.

A sense of humor is vital in life. Taking ourselves too seriously everyday and not stopping to "smell the roses," is taking away some of the very elements that destroy what you are trying to accomplish. We all make mistakes. We all face adversity. The key is not what we face but how we face it. For sure much of life needs to be taken seriously. However, realizing there are some things we can only adjust to and not completely change to our liking makes our life much easier than continuing to fight battles you can't win.

Don't be indecisive in life. There are many people who "beat a dead horse." If there are decisions to be made that are straight forward, don't put them off and let them "eat" at you. Make the decision based upon the facts you have and then move forward. Not being able to make decisions, especially small ones, indicate a lack of self-confidence and continual need for reassurance from others. Feeling satisfied and content with life decisions make fulfillment much easier to achieve.

Finally we need to "loosen up." We have to evaluate ourselves. What makes us as individuals happy? Go after what makes you happy in life because only then will you be moving toward a fulfilled life. Don't go after the same goals your best friend goes after. You are a different individual. Do not put yourself in a position late in life when you look back and find regret. Make each day count. Seek fulfillment.

ARTICLE 23

LEADING YOURSELF
AS WELL AS OTHERS

Some of the world's greatest leaders shared many leadership skills in common but one area that is not discussed often about these people relates to how well they led themselves.

A person's individual makeup, i.e. character, integrity, even physical health, determine much about the quality of leadership that person will display with others following his or her direction.

Being decisive in how you want to live your life is a key function of leadership. Making well thought out decisions, charting the consequences, both pro and con, and then abiding by that decision in your life is a true characteristic how not only you are directing your life but how you would direct others. Situations may be different but the core principles in your character will still be present.

People who are successful at what they do are also consistent in pursuing their goals. Leadership demands you be able to solve obstacles that will come your way and be prepared to face additional obstacles that will surely come about. In reality isn't that what life is all about? There isn't a day that goes by we all don't face one obstacle or another. Some more intense, others maybe not even so noticeable. Giving up or even settling for something less than our desired goal is not an option to successful people nor is it an option for a good leader.

Successful people are also those who can motivate and inspire themselves to keep on going. The great leaders can inspire and motivate others. But in order to do the latter, they must be able to do the former.

There is nothing more difficult than forcing you to do something when you don't feel well, want a day off, or attend a family function. It is the ability to force the shot, motivate you to get up and get going that makes the difference between success and mediocrity. Successful people sacrifice to get to their desired goal. They work when they are sick, tired and sometimes even when it means giving up valued time with friends and family.

This type of motivation is what inspires others to want you to work for them, to be part of their social and professional circle. And this is the type of inspiration that others see when you become their leader.

Finally how well you communicate with others is vital to a successful leadership role. If you look at the career of a successful person a key point in that individual's life is those closest to he or she knew where that person wanted to go and achieve in life. Communicating with others, being clear they understand the doors you want to open and the paths you want to take in life make leading yourself to a defined goal much easier. The same is true in leadership of others. You must be able to communicate your desires to others you are leading. Good leaders must be able to relate not just generically to an overall group, but on an individual basis as well, what the desired goal is.

Industries and businesses across the world have failed, not because of the employee performance itself, but because the employees simply didn't understand what they were supposed to do. As a supervisor, a teacher, a coach or anyone else who is placed in a leadership position, in order to be successful for yourself or your company, you must be able to communicate with both your staff and your superiors.

Just as communication is critical in living your life, raising your children, having a successful marriage, etc., communication is critical in leadership dictating whether failure or success results.

ARTICLE 24

SELLING YOURSELF
TO YOURSELF

Most of us have been in some sort of resume writing class at one time or another. The ultimate goal of any resume is obviously to sell yourself to the employer to get the desired job.

When we develop a resume we put down any and everything we think will stand out to whoever you want to see it. So we put past education, work experience, wherever we did volunteer work and anything else we think relevant to getting the job. Most of the time when we present a resume it has already been reviewed by friends, even former employers. There are repeated checks for grammar, spelling and a double checking of various dates where we may have graduated, worked or attended school.

But did you ever take time to write a resume to sell yourself to the most important person in your life.....you? That's right; the most important person in your life is you. That's why it is imperative that you buy into you!

So if you made out a resume trying to achieve the one goal of making you like yourself how would you do it? I always told my students that if you wouldn't hire yourself why would anyone else want to hire you?

What kind of education and experience do you have that you are proud of? What achievements and goals have you accomplished over your life that you are proud of and make you proud you are you? Have you been a good father, mother, husband, and wife? Have you dealt with adversity and come back stronger than ever?

Most importantly do these qualities and attitudes reflect the person you want to be? Do you include a plan, not for further academic education, but a plan for continual improvement of your life? Are you an individual with a well controlled temper and are open-minded to new challenges but not too naïve to be taken advantage of? Can you admit when you are wrong, take constructive criticism and apply it where needed?

And finally, what kind of a reference letter would you write to yourself saying why you like yourself? Could you sell yourself, the type of person you believe you are, to yourself?

TOTAL QUALITY LIFE MANAGEMENT

There is something to be said about quality of life. Unfortunately we many times never hear about quality of life until some dramatic event occurs with a loved one where a major decision must be made by family members based on the quality of life that loved one may or may not face in the future.

The business and industrial world have long relied on a variation of the Total Quality Management (TQM) concept, a process developed for success on a long term basis using various data, strategy and communications to integrate together creating a positive, productive and profitable enterprise. What I have tried to do is take the basic elements of the TQM concept and apply them to our individual lives.

The ultimate goal of life, just as in business, should be long-term success. The process for insuring this success should be continually developing, utilizing various data, strategy and communications with periodic review where changes are needed as circumstances in life change.

I want to mention five basic steps I have developed for the Total Quality Life Management concept. These steps need to be implemented together for full effect, not necessarily in an overwhelming manner that could cause discouragement but in a time-frame best suited for each individual.

To begin, the entire process must be participant-focused and you are the participant. We as human beings actually determine the quality of our lives. Before you can begin any journey you must know your ultimate destination. Where does the road map lead to? I often ask my students where they want to be in one, five or ten years. Only you can determine that destination but if you allow someone else to plan your life, set your goals, you will never achieve the satisfaction and fulfillment you deserve.

Make your decisions based on facts not on desires. The ultimate goal of Total Quality Life Management is to achieve the desires you want in life but you must make the decisions to reach that goal on facts not on desires. You must know where you are now. You must know what current conditions and resources as well as obstacles are present in your life and base your decisions on how you move forward on those facts. Perhaps the best way to say it is, "realize what current reality is to successfully move to future reality."

Consistently strive to improve your plan to achieve your goals. Life changes every one of us every day. No matter how well-developed, intensely researched or good intentioned, all plans change. And of course there is no way we can predict with total accuracy what the future holds. What we can do is keep ourselves in a constant mind set that "everything can change so don't let change derail your ultimate destination." Do not be afraid to make changes in your route to your goals; just be certain you don't change your goals along the route.

Develop a strategic and result-oriented approach. Successful coaches will tell you winning aren't possible without a well thought out game plan. It is all about practice, trial and error. Each opponent requires a different strategy. What plays do you practice to get the best results and what plays provide no positive results? As with sports, strategy and successful results are critical in life. Each one of us must develop a strategy that will provide positive results for us. And the strategy must be well thought. Developing and implementing a plan for Total Quality Life Management cannot and should not be done overnight. Your life deserves your time, your patience and your best effort. Remember if you don't give your life the time and respect it deserves who else will?

Finally communication is as critical in developing a quality life management plan as any other element of the process. Honest communication with yourself is the key. Only you know how well the process is going. You don't have to be honest with your family or friends but only you know for sure if your plan for a total quality life is moving forward and if you are happy with the progress. Honest and open communication with yourself is a key to a successful life no matter what direction you want your life to take. Don't develop the plan you think your friends want you to develop, instead develop the plan you want to develop.

ARTICLE 26

NEGOTIATING WITH YOURSELF

If the truth be told, most if not all of we negotiate with ourselves each day. We talk ourselves into and out of everything. And if we stop to think about it, it would probably shock us what we give up just because we can't win an argument with ourselves.

We tend to cave in to ourselves easier than we do to anyone else we negotiate with. If you don't believe me, ask yourself how you keep eating one more piece of candy, an extra ice cream bar, why you took the rent money and went on a weekend vacation, etc.? Scary isn't it? We give in to ourselves so much more than we give in to anyone else.

Negotiating with ourselves is also what helps us seek treatment not just for addiction but for physical issues as well. We negotiate with ourselves to determine whether we want to keep living the same lifestyle or whether there is a better way. It is a tough negotiation. Usually during those periods very little if any support is trying to convince you to side on the treatment and recovery decision. The same situation occurs many times for the negotiation you have with yourself over whether to go to the emergency room for physical illnesses, injury, etc.

I believe it is fair to say the toughest negotiator we will ever face is ourselves. Career decisions are made based on how we negotiate with ourselves. Do we want to go away to school? Do we want to change our lifestyle, leave our comfort zone? Do we want to be a doctor, lawyer, police officer, fireman, and accountant? All of these decisions are made through intense negotiation with ourselves. Sure we get input from others but the primary debate is within ourselves.

The internal negotiation also applies to whether or not get to get married, have children, even make critical or sometimes life-changing decisions for family members. Negotiation with ourselves is one of the most frequent and the most important negotiations we will ever have.

When negotiating with ourselves there is some tips that might make the process more simplified but not any less important. To begin, realize you are negotiating an issue that will have an impact, possibly a permanent impact, on your life. In other words, respect yourself during the process. Just because you are trying to make a decision, don't take it lightly just because it is you making the decision.

Even though the decision you are negotiating with yourself over may be personal or only affecting you, be certain you have objectively thought through all the pros and cons. Don't fall into the trap of putting more emphasis on what you can easily see as the positives and not give equal time to considering the negatives. Remember, you can fall in love with a beautiful house, sign the contract, and suddenly not just the loan payments but also the utilities, the taxes and the required upkeep to keep it "beautiful" all start popping up. Think about those types of possibilities for any issue you negotiate with yourself over.

Another point to keep in mind when negotiating with yourself is to give your decision some time. For sure there is a tendency to want to make a decision and move forward. But keep in mind that as with any negotiation with another person or company, there is needed time to consider all alternatives. Some alternatives do not materialize overnight. Lay out your game plan, particularly if this negotiation with yourself is going to be a life-changing long-term decision. The result of the negotiation is what is important not the time taken to make it.

ARTICLE 27

FRESH THINKING LEADS TO FRESH ATTITUDE

Over the years I have never been ashamed to say I have various mentors and also organizations that I not only admire and respect but who I also take pride in sharing some of their thoughts, ideas and attitudes that have helped frame my personality, values and general out look on life.

One of the organizations, for which I will always be deeply indebted to is the Pacific Institute located in Washington State. Its founder, Lou Tice, a former high school football coach, educator and motivator is someone I wish I had known and had been able to learn more from before his passing a few years back.

Mr. Tice spent his career motivating young people and also exploring new ideas and finding new avenues to get old ideas rejuvenated into today's society.

One of the basic premises of the Pacific Institute is its commitment to bringing fresh thinking into our life. As pointed out on the Pacific Institute's website, thepacificinstitute.com, fresh thinking unleashes creativity and allows you to respond to today's ever-changing environment.

As also pointed out, resistance to change, slow responsiveness, "can't do" attitude and lack of motivation are signs of a mindset issue. It is this resistance to change and refusal to try new ideas thinks out of the box that has led to complacency not only in our professional but personal lives.

As counselors, pastors, teachers or coaches, one of our most important challenges is to help people construct their attitudes and lifestyles in a direction that will lead to success. Mindset is a process that takes a lifetime to develop and thus it is almost certainly going to take a tremendous effort to change. Sometimes dramatic events will help convince others that maybe a change is needed, a different way of looking at life. Included are births, deaths, job losses, natural catastrophes such as tornadoes, hurricanes, flooding. Also to be included in changing a mindset is religion. Being reborn to serve for Jesus Christ or the conversion from one religious faith to another can lead to an acceleration of a changing mindset.

My friends at the Pacific Institute like to call changing a mindset, "Unleashing our Potential." I couldn't agree more! Mindsets many times are the product of environment. Environment can often bring about feelings of inadequacy, hopelessness and status quo. Hence potential is only never considered, the idea of unleashing potential is never dreamed of.

As we look at our lives presently one question we need to explore is whether we have realized our potential and to develop an attitude of focus on what our potential could be. We always tell our students the future is theirs for the taking. It is the decisions they make in the present that will determine their potential for the future.

ARTICLE **28**

_____

COMMUNICATIONS CRITICAL TO SUCCESSFUL DEVELOPMENT

When we talk about basic life skills there are no doubt that the most important skill has to be communications. Our communication techniques are critical to success whether in the personal or professional arena.

In the early school years emphasis was placed on communication skills, speaking clearly, correct pronunciation and proper reading assignments. However, the elementary beginning of communication skills has not evolved into our adult lives as efficiently or formally. It appears that many problems both personal and professional that people encounter throughout their lives has to some extent resulted due to lack of communications effort.

Effective communication skills must center on certain principles. Primary in those principles is the respect you show the individual you are talking to. I always encourage my students to look at the person's eyes as you are talking. You don't have to stare but make eye contact. Eye contact shows interest. When I teach job interviewing skills I make my students do a practice interview in front of a mirror. What they see in the mirror is what the person interviewing them sees. Notice where your eyes are, notice where your hands are. Do you look relaxed, scared or simply not interested?

All of these tendencies you see in the mirror indicate the kind of respect you are showing the person you are talking to.

Listening is a key principle in communications. When I was coaching there were many times I would give a player instruction on how to do a certain play, where to throw the ball, etc., and I could tell by the look in the young man's eyes I wasn't close to getting his attention. How many times do you actually listen when people are talking? Remember that person talking to you sees your physical reaction to what he or she is saying to you. If someone is talking to you and can tell you are not listening, it is taken as an insult. You are not caring what they are saying. Keep in mind that happens in many personal situations, maybe more so than business. Marriage counselors in particular will tell you that not listening to what the spouse is saying, not necessarily doing what is being said, but just listening to what is being said, is cause for the beginning of many divorces.

Another sad but true fact that has become dramatically apparent is not listening to what our children are saying. We are all guilty of not listening to our kids. There are a million reasons why we don't but the bottom line many times is that when something really bad might occur it can be traced back to something a parent should have listened to. This isn't always true and a guilt trip by the parents shouldn't always be the result but lack of communications with our kids is a major problem in our society today.

People like to hear their names. When you talk to someone, try to mention that person's name in the conversation. Think about what occurs when you hear your first or last name mentioned. We immediately "perk up." Hearing our name mentioned makes us pay attention. And when you say a person's name they pay attention to what you are saying. Mentioning the name of the individual you are talking to shows you are respectful, care about that person enough to remember his/her name and draws their attention to exactly what you are saying.

Try very hard not to let a conversation end without a result of some sort. Whether the conversation is personal or professional, do not let that conversation appear to be the last you have. In business conversations the technique is going to revolve around the project of discussion but always make a point to let the other person know you would like to schedule another meeting to either update current information or explore other opportunities to make a business deal work. Never let a potential business partner believes you are not flexible or not considerate of his/her position and situation. Mention a future date and time to get together again. This may or may not always work but the most important result is you have let the other party know you are interested, want to develop a relationship and work together for a profitable situation for all parties. The best way to say this is "put the ball in their park!"

Personal conversations should also never end without a result. People, especially friends, like to be reinforced that they are your friend. When you go to lunch, dinner, or a ballgame with a friend, make sure you set up another time to talk. Always telephone, email, or talk face-to-face. The method is not as important as is the fact you are making the effort. This lets your friends know you care, you value their friendship, their opinions and their lives being part of yours. By never ending that conversation without making sure another get-together is set, your friends listen and you will listen. Again, no conversation business or personal can ever be sure of effective communication with letting the others in that conversation know you want to talk or meet again. Effective communication results when all parties know they are the concern of those they are trying to communicate with.

Finally I think it is worth mentioning that on our global stage, successful communication is being demonstrated as the difference between successful economies, improved technologies and the difference between war and peace. Today it is more critical than ever that whether it is personal or business, effective communications between parties for success is critical before accusations and rumor destroys our society.

ARTICLE 29

CREATING YOUR PERSONAL DEVELOPMENT PLAN

In the professional business world, industry and education, employees are expected to create and follow a Professional Development Plan. Included in the plan is a map of where the employee currently is from a salary, position title and responsibility standpoint. The plan is basically a liquid instrument that enables both management and the employee to see where the employee is and where he or she needs to go from a professional training standpoint to move to another level or maintain the position currently occupied.

In life it is necessary to create a personal development plan. Many of us actually do have such a plan although we most likely don't have it written down.

So why do we need a personal development plan? What is personal growth? Do you see yourself better off today than you were a year ago? How about do you see yourself better off today than you were a month ago?

One of the primary lessons I was taught as a coach was that no matter what game plan you developed you had to be flexible enough to make changes when necessary and to also admit to yourself some of the plans you may have developed just were never going to work.

Developing a personal development plan involves knowing where you are now! And it also involves you realizing where you want to be in the future. Set small periodic goals systematically with a series of steps to reach those goals. Move forward slowly one step or goal at a time.

An unfortunate fact for many today is "planning" not being in the vocabulary. "Flying by the seat of your pants," or just living day to day and worrying about tomorrow when it gets here, are attitudes that are too very common in our society.

Personal development planning is another key to success. It therefore is to be included as a tool in the process for developing high self esteem, self-respect and moving forward with a productive life.

When you attempt to write down a personal development plan you will find yourself looking at a picture of what you want yourself to be. As you begin to develop ideas of not only what you want to do but how you want to get where you want to go, you feel yourself in a more positive vain. You will begin to develop an inner confidence that you are going to make it. You will begin to feel stronger emotionally, feel more determined and most importantly start believing in yourself. As you go back and review the plan, which can be done as frequently as you want, you will start to make little changes, develop methods for attaining the goals you've set and start gearing your life away from those elements that are keeping you from reaching your goals.

One note of caution however is not making any dramatic change in your plan at one time. Let the changes evolve as your life begins to move more toward the direction you want it to. Immediate and direct changes without giving some reasonable time for your personal development plan to start working will reflect more of an attitude of wanting to stay in the same position in life as before the plan was ever conceived. It needs to be very clear that creating the personal development plan is the easy part but making it work is where the real effort and dedication begin.

Finally it is important to have some support system as you develop and strive to implement your personal development plan. Those you are sure will be supportive of you changing your life into a positive and productive person certainly need to be included in your plan development process as might your counselor, pastor or even your supervisor.

Personal development plans are not a one-time assignment. To be successful they must also be fluid, have the ultimate goal of your happiness and your utmost focus.

HOW WE COPE
WITH WORRY
DETERMINES HOW
WE COPE WITH LIFE

Dealing with anxiety, anticipation of the unknown, or simply put, worry is the single most shared part of everyone's personality. From the rich to the poor, from the old to the young, from the honest to the dishonest, worry is fundamental as a personality trait.

Worrying has no preference when it spreads its infection. Some of us handle worrying with ease, making preparations throughout life to cover any possible conflict or potential circumstance that could be reasonably anticipated. People go to college to get jobs that will lead to a secure and productive future, they search for the right mate to share their lives with, they make what they believe to be the proper financial investments, live within their budgets and eat healthy and exercise regularly.

There are others on the opposite extreme who boarder on the neurotic. Whatever situation life hands them they immediately focus on every possible thing that could go wrong and not just wrong but how wrong! These people don't sleep nights; when they do sleep they don't get rest. These individuals also are so preoccupied with their obsessions of everything going wrong they actually drive friends and family away. Some people become so compulsively obsessed with worry they actually need medication and counseling to help control their anxiety.

Fortunately most of us fit into the middle of those two extremes. There is much to be said about preparing for life. Looking at and realizing the potential for problems and the need to prepare for those possibilities is a good quality but there is something to be said about being obsessed with the future and not enjoying the present.

With regard to the compulsion to worry about every detail in life, it is obvious both mental and physical health is going to suffer. These people who worry to such a degree not only don't enjoy the present they dread the future.

Let's be clear that worrying to a degree is both helpful and natural. Worrying does have its place in solving problems. Worrying within reason will force you to take action, either the right action or the wrong action, but worry is a motivator. There are many times that worrying actually allows you time to evaluate various options for solving a problem. Most problems of any magnitude definitely need time for evaluation to find a successful outcome.

The idea that anxiety and worry dominate both your conscious and subconscious thoughts is a recipe for both physical and mental health disaster. Intense worry actually only increases the problems you are concerned with because you are not rationally approaching the issue. The anxiety and the tension within your body affect your thinking process and your reasoning suffers dramatically.

Different counselors and psychologists will give you different ideas on controlling worry, everything from meditation to different prescriptions. I would like to recommend before you go down any roads that are both expensive and controversial to ask yourself three questions and answer them as honestly as you can: (1) Is the problem you are worrying about something that is current or something that you are anticipating? (2) In your honest opinion is there really any chance the problem you are worrying about will ever actually happen? (3) Is this a problem that in reality is out of your control?

You must be honest with yourself in answering these questions. So should the intensity of worry be great if you are only anticipating a problem? Is the problem you are worrying about something no one really has control over including yourself? These are just some ideas and thoughts you might want to consider before pushing out of your life people and events that could be very meaningful for possibilities that may never happen.

ARTICLE 31

ARE YOU GROWING TOWARD YOUR VISION?

There comes a time when you have to stop thinking and talking about doing something and start doing it, or as they say, "start walking the walk."

We all need to begin moving our visions toward reality. Whether you have a vision to be a great pastor, businessman or even a better parent or friend, you can only talk about it so long. Then two things occur: (1) those you keep talking about it with get bored and (2) you keep finding more reasons to not move forward.

Rick Warren, the senior Pastor at Saddleback Church in California says that the vision behind Saddleback Church would be nothing more than a vision without the steps of faith taken to plant, and then grow the church. With regard to faith, Warren points out that God rarely asks you to take leaps of faith, rather he encourages you to take small steps that grow larger as your faith grows larger.

It is interesting to look at God's word when we talk about motivation, improving self-esteem and confidence. God motivates people in many ways, faith certainly being one. The faith that God will lead you through the difficulties of recovery, job or family loss, illness or other misfortune is strong enough motivation for Christians to move forward with their lives.

There needs to be pointed out that many of us who speak at the seminars, write the columns and the books regarding motivation and self improvement all should recognize that faith is a primary tool used by God to motivate His people and that faith in God and the belief that He will lead us down the right paths is critical in any successful motivational program.

Today there are many faith-based addiction and alcohol recovery centers in towns all across the United States. Churches and community centers host evening meetings, there are weekend events with picnics, clubhouse activities and community service programs available but most all have the common denominator of a faith-based core.

There is no doubt that the first step in making a vision reality is the hardest. It is also the hardest step because it is what forces us out of our comfort zone. We must have that devotion to God and faith that He will lead us through to our ultimate vision before we can really get from home plate to first base.

ARTICLE 32

THE GIFT OF LEADERSHIP

We talk a lot about leadership and what it takes to be a successful leader. I have written on leadership styles, how leaders need to lead not to "boss." But one important element I have never touched on is a key to being a quality leader. And that element involves why you were chosen to lead.

We are all born with gifts from God. The thing that separates us from each other is how well we use or don't use those gifts and if we generate those gifts towards paths God wants us to take.

Being a leader can be extremely ambiguous. For example, as cruel and harsh as some of history's dictators and criminal kingpins were, they knew how to lead. Certainly they led by methods which were threatening, intimidating and divisive but they did lead and for many years, sometimes many generations, that leadership style worked. Were these leaders people God chose to lead or were they people who seized the moment, had their own ego and ambition blind them to the great benefits their gift would have been to society and indeed blind themselves from the actual beauty and love Jesus Christ could give them if they would have only followed His desires?

Leadership roles can be blinding. Leadership ability is a gift from God. But as with other gifts God gives us, leadership to can be abused, corrupted and cause permanent harm.

Another point to make about God giving us the ability to lead is that while many of us look at leading as being a supervisor or head of some company or group of employees, we tend to forget that God gives us the ability to also lead in our families, with our friends, even with strangers.

The recovery process is a typical example of good leaders leading others. And I am not talking about group leaders or counselors. The majority of people in recovery share in common the fact that one or maybe two others actually led them to the recovery process. Those people may still be in the recovery programs because of being led (although their desire to become clean was obviously a major factor as well) but they were led there by actual leaders, not necessarily trained by college or social media programs but through the grace of God. God chose those people to lead others to a path for recovery. These leaders followed God's desires and are now reaping the rewards, joy and satisfaction of knowing they served the One who gave them the gift.

One of the things I have learned in recent years is that schooling, degrees, attending lectures and going to the right meetings have so much less to do with being a successful leader than humbling myself before God, confessing my pride and asking Him to cleanse me of my sins and move forward honoring Him by using the gifts He has blessed me with.

The gift of leadership is truly a gift. A gift we need to appreciate and share.

ARTICLE 33

OVERCOMING OBSTACLES TO SUCCESS

When we begin to measure the success we have achieved in life, we immediately begin to look at the obstacles that we think stopped us from being even more successful. Actually sometimes we really dwell more on what we think caused us to not move further in our lives or careers than being happy and appreciative of those goals and accomplishments we have achieved.

As we begin to set the goals for our lives we need to develop the realization that successful achievement will require hard work, dedication and possibly even a complete change of lifestyle. The old saying, "nothing comes easy," is a fact when mapping out a set of goals and objectives that will lead to a successful life.

An acceptance of the concept that the only true obstacles in life are those we place on ourselves is a primary tool in the quest for successful life.

The fear of failure is, in my opinion, one of; if not the strongest of obstacles we face on a day to day basis. Whether it is because of either having an ego too large to ask for or accept help, the belief you are being seen as inadequate or imperfect, and the idea that others may perceive you as weak, feed the fear of failure you have to succeed.

Effort and desire are obstacles to overcome if you are to maintain a healthy and successful life. Any worthwhile endeavor requires enthusiasm, dedication and a strong work ethic. Lack of effort, laziness, both mentally and physically are all obstacles that need to be dealt with when moving toward a successful life. How strong are you mentally? How disciplined are you? These are questions that need to be examined and answered before success will be in view.

Ask yourself what kind of commitment you are willing to make to bring your goals to reality. What are you ready to sacrifice to achieve your goals? Are you ready to give up your social life, time with friends and family, work different hours and possibly temporarily take a night job you hate because you may need to get extra training or education? Are you willing to sacrifice vacations, ballgames, etc.? Lack of commitment is an obstacle you must overcome in order to move forward.

A deeply embedded behavior of apathy can be a difficult obstacle to overcome. Success does not just come because you sit there doing the same thing day after day and expecting the world to open up new doors to you. "Making waves and "going with the flow," are not ways to move forward in life. They may keep you popular for a time, but the very fact you don't want to make waves and ask for a promotion, change of job duties, etc., indicate you are a follower and not a leader. They indicate you want decisions made for you and not by you!

We all face obstacles in life. But some are similar and for most of us, the way to overcome those obstacles is similar. It is up to us to take the initiative, to dare to live our own lives.

ARTICLE 34

ADDICTION, RECOVERY, FREEDOM, FAITH

Over the years of writing this column, we have been able to have a front row look at how people handle life. We have seen and talked about life problems from emotional and mental health to physical health, birth and death. Throughout these years we have watched and tried to help others guide their lives in the direction they desired for success. And we have learned so very much about how the real world operates and getting out of the glass "Bubble" by talking with students, clients and colleagues who bring us the realities of life from various backgrounds and cultures.

Moving forward it has become apparent that certain "demons," if you will, have moved their way through all areas of society. The very issues we try to help people with in improving their lives are continually challenged and we have to find ways to fight back.

Addiction, regardless of alcohol or drug, has worked its way into most every one of our lives in one way or another. Though group and individual counseling, with prescribed medications have worked well in the continual combat with this problem, it is apparent and urgent that we as counselors, mental health professionals, pastors, family members and friends look for more intense weapons.

We all know that addictions have certain things in common: they provide a form of escape, they serve the purpose of removing a person from his/her true feelings, and they usually always involve pleasure and result in some form of psychological dependence.

Recently I read an article about what causes the growing threats to our society: Sin? Is this a disease? Is this a choice? Is this genetics? I frankly vote for all four. The genetics issue continues to grow as more and more "crack" babies are born each year. The alarming truth is that as these babies grow into adult hood and have their own children, we really don't know how the genetic traits will be affected. This isn't to deny the fact that there are also many children born to alcoholic mothers and fathers as well and research continues to show negative effects of alcoholic parents on newborns.

Disease and choice seem to come one after the other. HIV infection, as well as other experimentation with drugs, causes long-term health care issues. These issues are both physical and psychological.

With regard to sin, we know for sure that Satan, like any other thief comes to steal, kill, and destroy but we also know that Jesus came to bring life and bring it abundantly. We certainly know that as we continue this uphill battle for our future generations' existence that we have to remain highly informed and determined to persevere. As we must stay clinically strong we must also increase the reliance on a strong faith and foundation in Jesus Christ as Savior and Lord.

Although the battle for freedom of addiction is fierce and fatal, with Christ as Savior and Lord, we realize in His power He can overcome and win this war, not just this battle. When we as counselors, teachers, family members or friends humble ourselves and ask for His divine grace and help we are using the strong weapon of Faith to help bring the methods of recovery and freedom from dependence on these "demons" into reality.

Faith-based counseling as well as clinical counseling needs to be combined and utilized by pastors and counselors alike in this horrible and deadly war on our culture and future.

ARTICLE 35

BELIEVING IS NECESSARY TO ACHIEVE

As faith and belief is critical for salvation, faith and belief is also necessary for achievement of life goals.

Most definitely we must have faith in God and the belief that through Him anything is possible. But keep in mind that as we work toward our career goals we need that faith to be as strong as ever.

God guides us through our career cycle as well as our personal cycle of life. Faith is what determined some of the most dramatic events of our generation. For example, when Allan Shepherd first orbited the earth it was not just his faith that made him be able to endure the practice times, study time, and intense physical fitness diet and routine necessary for the trauma that his body would face, it also took his tremendous faith that the mission could indeed succeed.

The Invasion of Normandy was another great example of faith. From President Roosevelt to all the allied military generals to the soldiers in the invasion, there was one major common factor: they all had faith the invasion would work, and with all of the horrible loss of life that occurred the faith of the American people, the military and our allies that the invasion would succeed prevailed and the war in Europe began to turn to a decisive victory for the United States.

History is full of many other great stories of faith. There are many stories involving people facing deadly disease or major surgeries but their unwavering faith in God and belief they would survive brought them successfully through their trials.

Faith is coupled with the belief in God. We demonstrate our faith and love with our communication to God through prayer. It is through prayer to God and the belief that God can and will answer prayer that continually leads our lives. We all pray to God for different things. How much prayer do you think was involved when the United States put a man on the moon for the first time? How much prayer do you think was involved when the Apollo 13 astronauts we stranded in space for several hours and how much prayer do you think is involved when the doctor tells a young man that his wife is in serious trouble delivering their first child and the situation is life threatening.

The point I am trying to make is that no matter what goals we strive for, either personal or professional, faith or belief in God are necessary, more necessary than all the formal education and motivational programs can ever be.

Pastor Rick Warren says that faith is visualizing the future. It believes before you see it. Having a strong faith in God and a belief that your needs will be satisfied is a visualization that success can be yours. You just have to believe to achieve!

ARTICLE 36

REACHING SUCCESS AND FULFILLMENT

We all know that sacrifice is critical in achieving success and fulfillment not just in career but personal life as well. The most common denominator for requiring sacrifice is that our lives are already moving along in one direction or another and in order to re-direct our lives we first have to determine what we want to change or give up in order to move out of our current comfort zone and aim at the new goals for success.

I try to give my students some basic points that they need to consider as they strive to move their lives in the direction they want and to realize that although none of these points are particularly easy to achieve they must also occur at their own time-table and not try to press to much sacrifice or change at one time. Everyone's life is different therefore everyone's circumstances are different. Just because you are not moving at the pace your friend may be doesn't mean you are doing anything wrong. Success and fulfillment is a personal "thing" for each of us. Therefore although the basic principles moving toward success may be the same the time frames and methods to get there will most likely vary.

Remember, life is not without risk. Risk is the key determinant for moving out of your comfort zone. Keep in mind that the basic difference between successful and unsuccessful people is that unsuccessful people "don't live their lives they accept their lives." Successful people don't accept their lives as they are but strive to "live the life they want to live." Stepping out of the comfort zone is risky. Only you can determine if the risk is worth the possible result.

The old adage of "trial and error" is always going to be prevalent in moving your life in another direction. We all make mistakes, lots of them. We always will make mistakes, the issue is in terms of what we learn or do not learn from those mistakes. When you make up your mind to move your life in another direction you obviously have decided you are going to accept change. Sometimes change is not as dramatic as other times. An individual must make the determination that in order to change lifestyle, i.e. friends, habits, schedules, etc., all are going to be part of that change. And you will second-guess yourself over and over. We all have and will continue to second-guess ourselves on life-changing decisions. It is a normal process to wonder if you made the right decision or not. The question you have to answer for yourself is, how much second-guessing are you going to do before you either let it revert you back to your old comfort zone or whether you "file" it in your mind and continue to move forward.

You must eventually determine what fulfillment means to you. Does success and fulfillment mean to you being accepted and respected by others or does it mean being accepted and respected by yourself? Sometimes I look at this like the "keeping up with the Jones" theory. Is success determined by how you believe others perceive you or by how you perceive yourself? And I think that comes down to a values issue. As we go through life we constantly find our values tested. There isn't one of us who can say that in one way or another at least one of our core values does not get tested in either a small or large way each day.

It seems to me the real key to reaching success and fulfillment in life must revolve around how we live with ourselves. Not necessarily physically but certainly emotionally. We all tend to get wrapped up in this idea that it's what others think of us: family, friends, co-workers, etc. that make us a success and living a fulfilled life. But we need to be careful that as we plan our route toward a new successful life that we develop certain guidelines or values that are mandatory for us to be happy. Do not set up a lifestyle, no matter how financially rewarding or peer impressive, that it ignores the very values and visions that got you started toward living the life you want to live and not the life you felt forced to accept. If you do then you will still be living a life you are being forced to accept and you will always be searching for fulfillment.

ARTICLE 37

STANDING FOR THE TRUTH IS NEVER TO BE ASHAMED OF

Over the last few weeks I have been going through some re-evaluation of various facets of my life, professional and personal. I have always been very proud of the fact that I have always tried to do the right thing whether in the classroom, politically or in the business world. As we get to certain points in our lives its natural to look back and see both the mistakes and the good things we've accomplished and then take a look at where we want to go in the future and try to develop the best pathways to get to that destination.

Standing for the truth, no matter what position it puts you in publicly I have always believed is the best path toward any destination. The Bible says in 1 Peter 4:16, "It is no shame to suffer for being a Christian. Praise God for the privilege of being called by His name." Sometimes the truth does not always appear to be the easiest answer but we need to realize it is always the best answer.

We have in our society came to a place where if we don't get approval of certain people in our lives or get the approval of certain people we want in our lives, we will never be happy. I believe that in itself is the very reason we have so many unhappy people in our society today.

Standing by our basic Christian principles is a key to success. The values system has tremendous influence on how well we will succeed both financially and personally. Every one of us makes mistakes and we always will. Making mistakes is not breaking away from core values but it is part of living. When I facilitate my recovery groups in alcohol and addiction, I try to emphasize that relapse is part of the recovery process. In the same way, mistakes are part of the life process. You can relapse or you can make mistakes. And guess what? You will! The key is not letting those relapses or mistakes restructure your life in an unhealthy and unproductive manner. You don't leave the recovery process because of a relapse and in the same way you don't quit living because you make a mistake.

If you haven't realized it yet, you soon will come to the notion that no matter how hard you try to impress some people, no matter how much you change your lifestyle to get them in your "corner," it's never going to happen. Actually they like manipulating you, getting you to do things you are unhappy with, know full well that are wrong, and could actually cause you harm or embarrassment.

Why give people the opportunity to manipulate your life? Is the insulting or name calling you may get going to cause you permanent harm? How about letting someone drag you into some internet argument or public debate that is pointless other than intended to embarrass you? How about someone calling you a name or labeling you because you've made a stand for Christ? None of these situations are going to because you harm. Actually your refusal to let these and situations like them influence your value of truth and doing the things you know are right will only make you stronger.

Standing for the truth is never to be ashamed of. It is a lesson we should be dedicated to instilling in our children. No one needs anyone's approval before they can be happy. Lying and manipulation is a road that is full of potholes, detours to nowhere, and will always have you driving your life around in circles wondering who you told what to and the only thing you will see pass you by is your life!

ARTICLE **38**

THERE IS ALWAYS
TIME TO QUIT LATER

I once read that the difference between faithful people and unfaithful people is that faithful people don't give up at the first sign of difficulty. They keep on trying. Faithful people are both determined and diligent. Basically they don't know how to quit.

This isn't to say that we all don't face many roadblocks in life. These roadblocks vary obviously and the consequences that have resulted with initial failures may have been so severe or traumatic that moving forward toward a particular goal or with a certain direction just doesn't seem to stack up evenly with the negatives. Sometimes those roadblocks don't always involve ourselves but may involve our families or our friends. It may be we feel the stress and pressure our loved ones may endure because of our efforts overshadows our own personal desires so a feeling of selfishness or self-centeredness encourages us to quit.

I think it is fair to say that success is a product of self-determination. It is a product of perseverance and how well you can "stay the course." And speaking from a coaching standpoint I can say that the "will" not to quit also involves a great support system. Coaches in all sports tell you the biggest disease that infects their locker rooms and dugouts is negativity. Negativity encourages you to quit. Negativity is a cancer that needs removed. Coaches who are successful immediately try to remove negative attitude players, successful business executives immediately try to remove negative employees and we in our personal lives need to not associate with those who are consistently discouraging and seeing only the bad. Jealousy and envy have no place in a successful life or career.

Here are two other points. First, don't let hate cause you to quit. Not necessarily hate for the goal you are trying to achieve, for really you don't hate the goal anyway, you are just frustrated at the process. Don't quit because you are developing a hate for those that may be causing you the problems involved with moving forward with your goals. Doesn't let hate of any individual be the fire that puts out your excitement and optimism about life? Forgiving isn't forgetting. Certainly remember who is trying to stop you or hold you back but don't let them win by burning a hole through you heart and sole with hate.

Also, remember you are never a failure at anything until you quit. Again let me point out that there are circumstances where maybe changing your methods, even if takes a longer time period, might be in order. Possibly stopping and reviewing how much you really want to achieve the goal or success you are looking for and eliminating some of those around you who are discouraging you every move because of envy or jealousy. And finally remember that there are many in your support system who want you to succeed, who don't want you to quit and will stand with you.

Finally a verse from 2 Corinthians 4:16-17, "That is why we never give up. Though our bodies are dying, our spirits are being renewed every day. "Our present troubles are small and won't last very long, yet they produce for us a glory that vastly outweighs them and will last forever."

There is always time to quit later.

ARTICLE 39

LEADERSHIP IS A FULL-TIME ROLE

Leadership is a term we hear everywhere, from sports to politics, from church to the business world. Phrases like, "leading from behind", "lack of leadership", and "born leaders," are heard everyday somewhere in our society.

When I hear people talking about leadership one of the first thoughts to cross my mind is whether we are talking about "temporary" leadership or "full-time" leadership.

It's been noticeable over the years in my career in business and government that there have been many people placed in leadership roles but to say they were leaders might be stretching it.

True leaders are people who are full time leaders. They lead not only at work but in most phases of their lives. Full-time leaders have many qualities that if not "built in," certainly become "molded" in their personality very effectively and quickly. People I consider "temporary" leaders are those who for whatever reason end up appointed as department heads, supervisors, or even advanced rank in the military but once the work-day is over go back to a life they are happier with, being told what to do and following others who are more than willing to lead them.

Temporary leaders in most cases are good people. They actually are people who know they shouldn't be leading, are not comfortable with any facet of leadership, but for reasons of money, job security or status accept a leadership role. Frustration usually steps into play and that seems to happen in critical times when true leadership is needed. When a temporary leader is faced with situations where a true leader is needed there is always a chance of disaster looming. In fact, businesses have closed, governments have failed and people have died because of temporary leadership.

True leadership is a full-time role. While I think there is something to be said for certain personalities being suited for a leadership role while others are not, the true leader also molds the God-given qualities with training, experience and a burning desire to lead. Many of the world's most influential leaders are also leaders in their homes, churches and communities. There seems to be a feeling of trust and confidence people have for those they want to be led by. I might add that the exact reverse can be seen with those of the temporary leadership model. The last thing people who are in need of leadership want is someone who demonstrates not just a lack of self- confidence in his/her abilities but also shows no interest in those they are leading or their welfare.

Being a full time leader requires not just the tactical leadership abilities for a specific job but also the tactical leadership abilities for managing self and others.

A few points I would like to make regarding true full time leaders and what you might want to emphasize if you are interested in being a full time true leader. First, a leader says "we". Leaders lead teams. No one wants to be part of a team if they don't believe they indeed are part of the team. It is a leader's responsibility to make every member feel like they are a crucial part of the team. The team approach gives immediate self-value to every member and it shows the team you as leader are part of it, both the successes and the failures. Keep in mind that people have to buy into the leader before the leader can be successful. No team leader can be successful or achieve any form of greatness if the team does not achieve the same accomplishments and the exact opposite is also true: no team can be successful or achieve any form of greatness if the team leader does not achieve the same accomplishments.

Another point of interest is that if you are going to be a team leader you have to "walk the walk." True leaders have to be compatible with those they lead. Being compatible with others increases the chances of trust. Trust is critical to any form of successful leadership. Team members also like to know their leader shares in their values. This doesn't mean everyone on the same team has to be the same religion or faith, but values such as honesty, caring, respect for self and others, need to be present for everyone to pursue the same goals. Additionally loyalty for each other is crucial. Having each other's back is imperative to a successful team. It is important to be there for each other. Team members need to know their leader is there for them both in the good times and the bad.

A motivational expert and mentor, John Maxwell likes to say, "Everyone communicates, few connect." Being able to connect with others is a key to development of a good productive team. Team members and team leaders need to be "on the same page." And with regard to connecting, team leaders need to respect the views of team members. This doesn't mean you have to try every idea every team member has, for that shows lack of confidence and inability to make decisions, but the team leader should give each member a chance to voice his/her thoughts and opinions and genuinely listen to them.

Finally I would say that true successful leadership is a full-time job. If you think about it, the very points we have been discussing are all points that we would want everyone in our life circle to have.....respect, good value system, responsibility. People acknowledge what they see. If you display the same personal qualities at home, with friends and on the job, then you will be a leader, a true leader in all areas. Remember that adding value to someone immediately causes that person to add value to you. And people value true leaders.

ARTICLE 40

THE DIFFICULTY OF
STAYING ON TRACK
IN ADVERSITY

Adversity is a continuing challenge for most of us. We just get through one problem or situation and another pops up. Adversity may not always come on us personally but have as great if not greater impact on us when it falls upon close friends or family members.

Adversity comes at us from all directions: From health, finance, family members, friends, and the list go on and on. The reality is that adversity is a threat anytime we love or care about anything or anyone. Adversity has a strong correlation with harm and we don't want harm to come to those we are closest to.

Pastor Rick Warren identifies three different types of suffering. First is "Common suffering?" Common suffering is universal. Everyone, Christians and non-Christians alike suffer the results of such disasters as hurricanes, tornadoes, flooding, fires, etc. Suffering of this type in the world is common to all.

Carnal suffering is a second type of suffering. This is identified as suffering you bring upon yourself from your own sin. Consequences of an immoral life: sexual permissiveness could result in sexually transmitted diseases, over-spending could result in bankruptcy, overeating could result in diabetes or high blood pressure. Stealing could result in prison. Basically carnal suffering is a result of poor decision making.

1 Peter 4:19 says, "Those who suffer according to God's will should commit themselves to their faithful Creator and continue to do well." The third type of suffering identified by Pastor Warren is suffering according to God's Will. Why does God want us to suffer: He is interested in our character more than our comfort? Suffering according to God's will deepens your faith, builds your character and will bring you more rewards in Heaven.

So it is fair to say that adversity raises its head at anytime and with anyone. How we come through that adversity is a reflection of how we lead our lives. Many people rely on their faith in God to get them through trying times. Unfortunately many other people turn to drugs, alcohol and other addictions to basically "hide" the adversity they are facing.

Realizing we can and will always be likely to face adversity in our lives is a certain start to dealing with it. Developing productive and healthy methods in advance to either prepare for or help prevent the intensity of a potential adversarial situation is a key to the energy and time you will spend on the adversity.

Remember that no matter what arrows are thrown at you, no matter what you suffer in this life because of your faith, God wants you to remain faithful to Him and keep on doing well for others. Adversity only wins when we surrender our values and principles, not when we let that adversity strengthen us.

WHAT IS YOUR SIGNIFICANCE?

If we were honest we would admit that every so often we tend to question ourselves on our own significance in life. Most of the time, we do this when we are depressed. We may be going through some trauma or facing situations that are difficult that have no easy answer.

I recently read in one of Pastor Rick Warren's essays that your real significance in life comes from serving others. As ministry is doing well for other people your significance in life can be determined by what good deeds you do for others.

Team work, doing things with others to achieve the same result, is part of developing your own significance in life. People learn from other people. No matter how good you may believe yourself to be for a particular task, you will be surprised how much you learn and improve on that task when performing it with others.

Giving other people the opportunity to work with you, to share their ideas, thoughts and beliefs is what give those people the feeling of you belonging in their lives or careers. This sharing makes you significant in the other people's eyes.

It is important to remember that how significant you are is not dependent on what you think of yourself, not how much money you make, what type of parties you attend or where you went to college but your significance is defined by your value to others in making their lives better.

Mom and Dad always told me that you need to think about others and not be selfish thinking about yourself. That is a philosophy I have tried to carry throughout life.

When you look at it, the idea of working with others as part of a team makes you significant in the other members' lives. How well you do your share, and even the fact that you are participating and doing your share gives you value to the others. You are working with them to achieve a common goal, a goal they feel they could not accomplish without you.

God has given all of us individual gifts. And as 1 Peter 4:10 points out, "Each of you has received a special gift to serve others." How well you serve others providing services and assistance is the determining factor in your significance.

I like to also believe that being a team player as opposed to being an individualist increases your significance in others eyes. Working with other people, being part of their lives and developing relationships and fellowship all enhance your significance. In being part of a team you can learn the values of forgiveness, faithfulness, love and unselfishness which are all admirable qualities that improve your significance with others. Most likely the way we develop and maintain relationships with other people is one of the keys to having a successful and productive life. Our significance is not based on how we serve ourselves but instead is defined by how well we serve and live with others.

In closing, remember Ecclesiastes 4:9-12, "Two people are better than one, because they get more done by working together. If one falls down, the other can help him up. But it is bad for the person who is alone and falls, because no one is there to help. If two be down together, they will be warm, but a person alone will not be warm. An enemy might defeat one person, but two people together can defend themselves, a rope that is woven of three strings is hard to break."

ARTICLE 42

MEN'S GROUPS

In the last month I have began a new challenge: facilitating men's focus groups. Over the years I have spoken to various different groups, i.e. political, business, education and religious, but all have been mixed with males and females. To be honest, the only men's groups I have ever been a part of were church men's breakfasts and bible study.

What we are seeing today is a serious need to develop more specialized groups for both men and women. Most specialized groups have one thing in common: they are small. Small can be a good thing. Meaningful exchange is much more likely to occur in smaller group settings. Margaret Mead, a well-known anthropologist was once quoted as saying, "Never doubt the power of a small group of people to change the world. That's about the only way it's happened in the past."

My biggest challenge in developing a men's group was to decide what topics and purpose the group would have. There are many variations of support groups: alcoholics, addiction, eating disorders, etc. The real question is what type of group will serve the best purpose.

I have established a few ground rules the first of which is to establish a group purpose. As I am going to be working primarily with addiction men in this group I felt the purpose would be to discuss not necessarily the addiction itself but rather the social and personal issues men with

99

addiction problems face such as difficulty in obtaining employment, housing needs, medical and psychological services. Also relationship issues with children, girlfriends and spouses. The entire stigma issue associated with addiction and how the individual is coping both physically and psychologically.

The next ground rule I set is to not ask for a long-term commitment from anyone. In order for this group to work I believe we need to let some exploration of the group without the pressure of commitment occurs. I really believe for the group to be successful it has to only have members that want to be there. I learned a long time ago as a teacher and coach that only students and players that want to be on a team or in a classroom will succeed in that environment. As a matter of fact if a small group has members that really don't want to be there it only makes it more difficult for those members who want to benefit.

My final ground rule is for me exclusively. I do not want to talk but to facilitate the members to talk. I tell every group I work with regardless of the purpose for the meeting, that the group is not my group it is our group. It is a team effort. In order to get free, open conversation everyone must feel they are on an equal level with everyone else. We are part of this group to work together, not for me to teach, instruct or advise.

As this men's group moves along, I realize the actual success will depend on how much value the group is to its members. If members of the group feel our discussions are valuable to them they will continue to come and participate. My early challenge as a facilitator is to make sure the group is valuable to the members and realize it is not about me but it is about all of us.

The best compliment any group leader or facilitator can get is to hear members of the group talking to each other about the value of the group and how it is supporting and shaping their lives. It's not what they are going to tell me, it is what they are going to tell each other that will determine how successful this group will be.

ARTICLE 43

BUILDING YOUR SUPPORT SYSTEM

Every one of us at one time or another needs some type of support from one or more people in our lives. Although there are many of us who like to "go it alone" there still will always be a time when we need to have someone else to either just "vent" to or ask for some sort of physical or emotional help and support.

Unfortunately in our culture we tend not to look at building a support system unless we are in some sort of trouble or difficulty. The reality is that we should be building our support system throughout our lives.

Inner circles of friends are usually the basic support system for most of us. These are the people we tell our deepest and darkest secrets to and they reciprocate. Sometimes however some of our closest friends in the inner circle of our lives are not necessarily the best support system for every issue we may face.

As most people who have been in one form of recovery or another will tell you, the best support systems many times are with people who have or are experiencing the same type of pain and difficulty you are. These individuals may not be your day-to-day inner-circle you work with, raise your kids with and even vacation with, but these are people who can and will give you the inner strength and understanding you need to get through the crisis you are experiencing.

Keep in mind that you can and should have support systems for different crises in your life. If you are someone who is having financial troubles, marital troubles or problems with your children, look to others who are going through those same issues. Believe me, you are not the "only" one.

So how do you find these support systems? Where are the best places to find these people? Obviously you can locate support groups for many different issues on the internet. But what we all really need is support systems with people we are comfortable with, meaning people we know.

Get to know the people you work with, go to church with, and go to the gym with. The best way in the world to find out what is going on in someone else's life is to just be "friendly." Smile, say hi, and talk about the weather. The next thing you know relationships begin to build. As they build you will learn more about them as they learn about you. Then you find that a lot of other folks out in the world share your same problems and obstacles. Sharing experiences with people who know what you are going through is support.

Being socially active doesn't mean you have to put your nose in every aspect of someone else's life but being accepted socially is a great start toward building several quality support systems you may need throughout your life.

One final thought. Family can and should be part of your support system wherever possible. But as we all know, family can also be a major reason you may need a support system. Family members sometimes see a thin line between not being asked to be part of your support system and being rejected. It is a dangerous tight-rope that many of us have walked in the past and will most likely walk again. The bottom line however is that we have to cope with and hopefully find a positive outcome to the crisis we are going through. Personal feelings of family and close friends are surely important but your own emotional and physical well-being must be paramount in your life in order to be productive and successful. Otherwise your life will be a constant conflict.

ARTICLE 44

BETTER TO WORK TOGETHER

Over the years I have always believed that team work is much better than trying to do everything by yourself. Teams just naturally get more things done correctly and faster.

In Ecclesiastes 4:9 God tells us, "Two people are better than one because they get more done by working together." This seems to tell us that as we go through life we are meant to work with others, do things with others. Not go through life alone.

So let's ask ourselves if we have been trying to accomplish too much work on our own. Another good question is why have we not wanted to ask others to work with us? What is the big reason many of us want to go it alone.

Team work brings so much more into our daily routines. Fellowship is impossible when you are alone. One of the reasons I believe many of us don't like to work with others is our desire to "do it our way." Being boss, being in charge. And when that attitude prevails it is hard to find a team or even one other person to rally around you.

How many times have you heard people say the only way they are satisfied with something is if they do it themselves? Amazing, narrow-minded and selfish, but people actually feel this way.

Life is not meant to go through alone. Granted there are many people we all know who really do go through life pretty much by themselves. Some, probably most, are older, i.e. A spouse has passed, children grown up and moved away, etc. I honestly have not read a lot of statistics on it but I have to believe that those of us, who go through life with someone, work with others, or at least experience fellowship with others on a frequent basis, have a happier life and higher self-esteem than if they were to go it alone.

Remember the saying, "Team work makes the dream work?" Human beings by nature are social people. Regardless of the culture or location around the world, human beings function better being together, working together.

If you are not part of a team, don't have much of or any social life, you might want to take a look at your lifestyle. Chances are if you admit it to yourself, you may find yourself depressed and not overly energetic. You should be with others, work with others, and being a part of life. That's what it's all about!

WHAT DOES MARRIAGE REALLY MEAN?

The answer to what marriage really means is certainly going to vary depending upon who you ask their experience or non-experience with marriage, their friend's marriages and their parent's marriages as well.

One part of the definition everyone should agree on is the sharing of life as one. Anytime there is a uniting of two or more into one, whether it is with businesses, churches, sports teams or human beings, a sharing or uniting together occurs. There are certainly some changes that occur, compromise and sacrifice to name two. But a coming together as one and to move forward as one is the ultimate goal.

So let's start by talking about coming together as one. Complementing and completing each other to the point you can have a better life as one rather than individually as two. It is important however to remember that even though you are bringing two lives together in a marriage each member is not required or expected to give up his/her identity and self-value. You still are an individual, with your values, morality, goals and expectations. No one should expect their spouse to give up basic values, integrity and individuality. Marriage is a coming together as one, not a controlling mechanism for one of the two.

Not being selfish is a factor in any marriage. Although you may have made very good and productive decisions in your life marriage brings something called consideration into the picture. The longer we stay single the longer we make decisions based on what we feel is best for us. It becomes a difficult challenge to start considering others in our decision-making process. Suddenly a decision isn't just what best for one but for both. Whether it is changing jobs, taking a vacation, buying a home or even having children, the decision is only going to be constructive if it is considered by both partners in the marriage.

Change is probably the most noticeable result of a marriage. Change in anything we do is always tense, questionable and causes a fair amount of anxiety. A major change in lifestyle is definitely going to produce its share of anxiety. Not spending as much time with friends, possibly not even seeing some friends as often, more emphasis on finances, and even a more sincere look at spirituality and faith are all changes we find as marriage comes into our lives. One piece of advice to people getting married, particularly for the first time is to remember it isn't just you trying to adjust to the change it is your partner as well. Working together and being supportive of each other helps make the change brought on in your life by marriage much easier and productive.

Finally I would add that marriage means not giving up on life but desiring to enjoy life more not being alone. It is a vehicle for us to develop ourselves in ways that should make us more efficient and productive as citizens, parents and human beings. Human beings were not created to be alone but to succeed best when we work together. Marriage gives us the opportunity to live our lives with someone else, to compromise and to understand other people's feelings and desires. It allows us to raise children, teaching them the values and principles necessary to lead our world into future generations.

Marriage is good times and bad. It's suffering through the bad to love the good. Marriage is not easy, not a project you work on once or twice a week, but rather it is a process that needs continual sincere love, support and dedication to each other. A good marriage is worth the mistakes, the affairs, the rejection, and yes the pain, if you work through them, compromise on them and always work to make tomorrow a better day for you both than today.

ARTICLE 46

———————

Choosing a
Role Model

Whether we realize it or not, we begin choosing role models as early as our childhood and continue to choose them as we move into adulthood. The question is, "is this a good idea?"

Obviously if we choose role models that are positive, productive and just plain good people, we have little to loose. But in today's society, especially with all the electronic social media outlets, it is easy to choose role models that can cause us more harm than good.

The whole idea of choosing a role model is to find someone that will inspire you to be a better individual, either socially, professionally, spiritually or a combination of all three.

Role models will move us out of our comfort zones. Choosing a role model means you have decided on a path or course of direction you want your life to move in. This also means you are developing your self-confidence and self-esteem. You are destroying scotomas and reaching out to be a more productive person to your family, your friends, your employer and society.

We tend to choose role models in many different methods and there is no exact science that applies to all of us. We tend to look up to people who were our teachers, coaches, pastors or parents. These are the people that usually guide us through the early stages of our lives. We see them more frequently and they have great influence on our adolescent years.

It is important to mention that a lot of this influence is not always positive. Psychology books are full of case studies where children who observe negative behavior tend to model that behavior as they get older. Jails, prisons, and cemeteries are full of examples.

In choosing a positive role model I think there are several considerations that need to be made.

First of all you should take an inventory of yourself. Where are you in your life? What parts of your life are pulling you down, causing you to feel worthless or helpless and what has led you to this point? Also look at your strengths and various characteristics you are happy with and want to retain. Keep in mind that this self-inventory may take a few days. After all, you didn't get in your current situation overnight so why would you expect it to change overnight?

Another challenge, possibly the hardest, is to determine the lifestyle you want to achieve. What are the attitudes and habits you want to develop into your life? Where do you want to go and how bad do you want to go there? How bad you want to get there will be the determining factor in the effort you will put forth.

Something else to remember when choosing a role model: whoever you choose had to overcome obstacles too! That person had role models also. They had challenges and adversity they had to overcome to get where they are. And, those same people are not just resting on their laurels.....they are still striving to both move forward and at the same time not slip back to where they once were....by using other role models in their lives. It takes work to get to where you want to go, and then harder work to stay there or move even further forward.

In choosing a role model, don't focus on any one particular individual at first. Take some time, don't let yourself take so much time you start avoiding making a decision, but done rush yourself.

Develop a list of characteristics, habits and goals you would like to achieve. Look for people who have those characteristics and that you admire for their accomplishments. Try also to learn about these people's failures and challenges. Look at how they got to where they are.

Another important point: Don't feel you can't model yourself after someone just because they have more financial wealth than you do. For example, most of us can't run out and buy a new car but if the person you are modeling yourself after has a new car, do the next best thing: take care of the car you have.....wash it, wax it, vacuum it, treat it in a way that if it were new you would treat it. Don't over-extend yourself into debt that will cause you even more problems. Start by improving and taking care of what you have.

One last point that I think is critical in finding a role model: Every one of us has our faults. No matter how successful we are all human. Do not become frustrated if your role model begins to show "kinks" in the armor. That does not mean the role model was a bad choice. It just means the person is human just like the rest of us. We all have our problems. The difference between success and failure is how we manipulate our problems into success.

Choosing a role model is an important part of our self-actualization process. It shows we are ready to improve ourselves, no matter how successful or unsuccessful we may currently be. It means we are ready to knock down more scotomas and move away from our comfort zones to a better life, personally and professionally.

ARTICLE 47

KEYS TO SUCCESS: HONESTY & TRUST

What value do you place on Honesty?

More than likely the answer most people give will be something like, "I hate a liar....., I hate cheaters......., I can't stand a thief...", and similar responses. But how honest are we really? And more importantly, how honest are we with ourselves?

When we talk about self-actualization, building our character and moving out of our comfort zones, it is critical to realize that if we are not honest with ourselves, if we can't trust ourselves, then we could easily be fighting a loosing battle.

If we are not honest with ourselves how can we possibly be honest with our families, our employers, our friends? Now, does this mean we have to go around revealing every little deep dark secret in our lives? Do we have to make our lives an open book? Do we have to paste our lives on some social media outlet for the whole world to see? The answer is obviously not.

But we do have to realize in order to move forward in life we first have to admit to ourselves our own limitations, faults and flaws. We certainly don't have to open our lives to the world but we must accept ourselves for what we are now in order to make the adjustments necessary to move forward in a positive direction in the future.

The question becomes, "how can I change something when I won't admit to myself something needs changed?" Self-actualization and positive self-growth revolves around the idea that in order to be successful you must be genuine and truthful to yourself.

Over the years I have had the opportunity to work with various alcohol and drug addiction groups. In order for any of the participants in these groups to be successful they must first admit they have a problem. They must be honest with themselves. Sure their clinicians and friends know their conditions but that is not important. What is important is that the individual know he/she has a problem, accepts it and truthfully and honestly wants to change for the better.

Here is another key point to remember: Honesty and trust breeds integrity! People who are honest and truthful with themselves are honest and truthful with others. They strive to live an ethical, productive and moral life. This is called integrity. They are respected by their families, friends, and co-workers and develop good positive reputations throughout their communities.

Before I got into management I found that many of my bosses really didn't want to hear the truth at work, they just wanted the work done. To some of them, hearing the truth meant problems! And problems meant the bosses had to work harder. The old saying, "I don't care what you have to do to get it done, just get it done", was the unwritten code each shift. The truth took a backseat to quality. Integrity was not a priority.

Later when I got into the management realm, one of the first things I did was call all of my department heads and staff into a meeting and made it perfectly clear, no matter how bad the truth may be, it better be brought to my attention. I may not have always liked what I was hearing sometimes, but I greatly appreciated the fact that my staff knew their work was important to me because I wanted it to be important to them. I wanted them to do quality work because it made them proud of there accomplishments. They knew being honest about work-related problems with management made the entire company better overall, the product was high quality and also the employee's self-esteem, pride and dedication blossomed. We developed a business known for it's honestly, trust and was regarded as a business of high integrity and trust in the community.

On a personal relationship basis, unfortunately honesty and trust have taken some major hits over the years. Today our society is divided on many moral and social issues. Marriages are strained by infidelity and mistrust. Churches are loosing membership and religion in general is questioned by many. Same-sex marriage, inter-racial marriage, living together without marriage and abortion are all issues people are trying to understand and cope with.

Counselors, pastors and even television reality shows can provide guidance to all of us in the many social issues of the day. But keep in mind that it is really all they can do.....provide guidance. The reality is we have to be able to be honest with ourselves, truthful with ourselves. Following along with the crowd is good if you honestly agree with the crowd. But if you are really honest and truthful with yourself, then you may not want to follow that crowd.

So in business and in our personal lives, honesty and trust is the key. If we are not honest with ourselves, the reality is we can't trust ourselves. And if we can't trust ourselves, self-actualization and happiness will only be a dream.

ARTICLE 48

EVALUATING OUR VALUES

Not too long ago, a close friend of mine, a retired teacher and coach, was telling our men's church breakfast group about why he finally gave up his teaching license and refuses to even substitute teach.

This gentleman taught for almost 40 years in the public school system, coached and officiated two varsity sports, and still today is regarded as one of these areas foremost authorities on youth leadership, sportsmanship and coaching strategies.

He told me that over the years he had been seeing deterioration in the attitudes of the kids. At first he said it seemed relegated to just certain groups, usually those whose families were regularly in trouble with the police or court systems. But that in the last several years it had continued to expand to those whose families were not in that category.

I think it is fair to say that many times the values our children display are the result of the values they see displayed. Much of this definitely comes from the family core but it also comes from our society as well.

Now here is something that many of you may disagree with: I believe society is not the blame for everything wrong in our family structure. It has a lot to do with it for sure, i.e. social media, television, news media, economics, etc., but to say society totally is to blame for our values systems deteriorating is not what I consider a valid statement.

I like to ask my psychology classes, "Who is Responsible for your Happiness." The correct answer is, "you are." I like to believe the same answer applies to who is responsible for our values systems.

As children, certainly we tend to imitate the actions of adults. If not corrected immediately, children will be mouthy, curse, even drink and smoke. Sexual permissiveness, even under age pregnancies is becoming the norm in many areas.

But when do we start taking responsibility for ourselves and our actions? When do we decide its time to admit there is a difference between right and wrong as well as legal and illegal?

For one, maturity is a factor. At what age do we mature? I don't mean sexually or even to the age we get a driving permit or can legally drink alcohol. What age do we become responsible for our actions?

There are some people who really never ever take responsibility for their actions. And they don't take responsibility for their children's actions either. When they or their children get into trouble, it's someone else's fault. They are really only upset about one thing: that they got caught. There is no regret of causing harm to someone else, stealing from someone else, even framing someone else for a crime they didn't do.

Basically what we are saying is they have no values system.

So how have values systems fell totally apart over the years? Do we place other factors in our life at a higher level than our own self-respect and self-esteem?

I believe that today more than ever, we need to evaluate or re-evaluate our personal values. If things are not going well in our lives, how much is really someone or something else's fault and how much do we bring on ourselves?

How far do we let economic and social events affect our attitudes toward life in general? There is no question that being unemployed or loosing a job you have had for many years is devastating and divorce or other negative personal events in our lives can create chaos and depression, but how far do we let it go before we totally change our personalities to the point we can't recover. Why do we let ourselves get to the point we say, "the hell with it," throw away everything that meant so much to us when we were successful and turn ourselves into something we may never recover from?

I believe that our inability to cope with life's day to day events is a major cause of our values systems collapsing. All of us are challenged more intensely today with family, the workplace, and even with friends than our parents and their generations ever were. The feeling of desperation and helplessness leads to an unhealthy values change. I also believe that our children reflect our attitudes and values. Thus, schools are having discipline problems more because they are a reflection of the personal life of the student.

We have to start adjusting our lives again. Lack of a values system is the result of no structure in our lives. We have no structure because we have no self-respect, no self-esteem and we are happy to blame others for our faults and setbacks.

Difficult as it is, looking at building up self-esteem, reminding yourself you are better than that, that you hold yourself to a high standard, and then developing goals to meet those standards, does indeed improve your values system. Meeting frustration and adversity head-on and dealing with it from a positive and direct approach gives you the feeling of taking charge of your life. It's time to move forward.

There is none of us that haven't faced adversity. Some of us do more dramatically than others for sure. But letting adversity take us over, throw out our values systems and stomp us into the ground causing us to become something we have never wanted to be, is something we must never allow to happen.

Just for Thought

Always evaluate and re-evaluate your values system. This is true especially in the bad times. Be conscious of your actions, how you treat people, how you treat yourself. Watch to see you are not slipping or falling further than you have to. Control your life, don't let it control you.

ARTICLE 49

THE PRACTICE
OF "LABELING"

A great part of my professional career has been spent working with people having special needs, both emotional and physical. As a result I suppose I have become extremely sensitive to labeling. I do take offense to people being harassed or bullied because of their race, creed, sexual orientation or any other part of their life.

Labeling has been a product of literally generations of prejudice, ignorance and plain stupidity. From the early days of our history degrading terms have been used to describe human beings because of the color or their skin or nationality. People being forced to ride in the back of buses, drink at segregated water fountains and not be permitted to stay at certain hotels.

Over the years others have been labeled with various insulting terms to describe their mental health conditions or their sexual orientation. And the brutal forms of labeling have not escaped those people who have physical disabilities either from injury or birth.

So why do labels exist? What inner urge do people have to label others?

Most people I have met who rely on labels for others have three common characteristics: insecurity, low self-esteem and are unable to cope with their own problems and faults.

Insecurity is the common characteristic in all bullies. People who are insecure in both their professional and personal lives strive to find anything possible to criticize others, to humiliate others and to harm others when possible.

People who have had multiple marriages and who have trouble keeping any one job for a long period of time refuse to admit they many times are the reason for their own failures and try to focus attention on others. These are the type of people who within ten minutes of meeting them are knocking their employer, the government, even their own families. They like to immediately strike out at others, labeling them as inept, unreasonable or always wanting a hand-out.

Insecurity breeds low self-esteem. Low self-esteem breed's loneliness and people who label others is lonely people. People who label others are lonely, sad and basically miserable each day of their life. The world owes them a living and it is backing out on its part of the deal.

Making excuses for not succeeding is a key with those who label. Being unable to cope with their own lives they strike out at others verbally and try to get others to laugh and ridicule as well. The laughter element is a form of power to those that label others. It builds up their confidence that they are somebody. It reality it only builds them up in the eyes of others who are just as bad.

The reality is labeling is cruel and is a mirror reflecting the personality of someone who sees his or herself as a failure at life trying to make others feel he or she is "somebody."

Any of us who strive for self-actualization, high self-esteem and a successful life do not involve ourselves in any pathetic practice of degrading others. Labeling is a complete negative in the process of self-actualization and positive personal growth.

ARTICLE 50

THE INNER CIRCLE

Who are the people closest to you in life?

We all have many friends and acquaintances in our lives. Some of these people are relatives, some are neighbors, others are co-workers and there are still others who we run into at ballgames, parties, or other social events.

Over the years many of these people come and go in our lives. There are some who we continue to see because of family or work, but for the most part, those who stay close to us are usually related to the family.

How many people in your life do you share your inner most thoughts and secrets with? This group, which is known as your inner circle, is usually very small. To some, it consists of only your spouse. To others, it may be one or two who have been close friends since high school or even before. You may have grown up together on the same street, played on the same ball teams, and maybe even dated the same people.

It takes a lot of trust and confidence in another person before most would bare their deepest thoughts. And keep in mind, this inner circle concept is not just one-sided. Most in these circles rely on each other. They actually rely on each other more they would a professional counselor, pastor or doctor.

Another point to make about those closest to us is that many times they are not necessarily that much like us. For example, it is not unheard of to have a doctor or lawyer only bare their souls to a person who may be a plumber, carpenter, or even someone who doesn't even have a job but has been a trusted friend their entire life.

I know of one situation where a friend of mine who has been elected to a high office only tells his inner most thoughts and desires to a guy who drives a garbage truck. It is a strong, long-lasting friendship that has endured since they were in grade school together. One of the strongest friendships I have ever known.

Over the years we all have told many of our closest secrets to people who have actually betrayed our trust and confidence. We thought we knew them but we really didn't. Many times when this happens, it is at an embarrassing time and usually results in the end of that particular friendship.

There really is no way you can set out to develop an inner circle. These groups tend to form over a life-time of association. These are people who we know we can go to and tell our deepest feelings, reveal our most bizarre thoughts and ask for advice that is valued more than from anyone else.

I keep thinking about an old saying that goes something like, "....don't get to big for your britches because I knew you before..." These are usually our inner circles. These are the people who know our lives, inside and out, but we also know their lives inside and out. There is no jealousy, not judgment, just plain honesty.

One other point to make is these inner circles don't always include spouses. As I mentioned earlier, to many the spouse is the only part of some people's inner circle, the only one that is trusted totally and completely. But many times, people with fantastic, long-lasting marriages never reveal every thought and desire to their spouse. It is not unfamiliar that when a spouse passes away, the other will find out many things they never knew when they run into one of their dearly departed inner circle.

People with high self-esteem and confidence, who pride themselves on being self-actualized and progressive, value their inner circle of friends deeply.

ARTICLE 51

DO YOU TAKE
CHANCES?

Do you consider taking chances or taking risks as gambling? And do you realize we all take chances and risks every day in life?

Taking chances or risk-taking, whichever terms you prefer, allude to the gambling process, and in many ways perhaps with good reason.

Someone told me once that he didn't see what the difference was in gambling for money when you gamble everyday. He says that getting out of bed each day is a gamble. Getting in your car and driving is a gamble, as is jogging, buying a new vehicle, even getting married. It is all taking a chance.

I like to think of it in terms of risk. There is responsible and needed risk and there is irresponsible and recreational risk.

For example, when you decide to get another job, have an opportunity for professional and financial advancement, there certainly is risk. You leave the comfort zone of your current occupation and enter a different arena. You are, or should be, aware of the risks, the chances for both success and for failure, but you move forward because the possible benefits for yourself and your family may out weigh the negative consequences that could result.

On a personal level, getting married or deciding to have another child, are certainly risks and there are many positive and also negative variables that must be considered. It is a responsible risk for sure and there is potential for many opportunities for great success as parents or for a successful marriage and there are also known and unknown risks for failure.

Recreational or irresponsible chances or risks include gambling for money, not taking prescribed medications, alcohol and drug abuse. To many people these type of chances or risks are worth the excitement or other "rush" they cause.

I do believe there are times and opportunities where risk is worth the chance. People who take responsible risks are people who are high in self-confidence and self-esteem but couple that will caution and precision. These individuals usually develop strategies for taking chances. They weigh the options but they also have a strategy mapped out for their lives. They know where they want to go. They know although the potential for failure is there, they are ready for the challenge and will persevere. These people have a "reason" for taking a chance. The reason for taking the risk is worth the chance it may not work.

Individuals who take irresponsible chances and risks are those same people who "fly by the seat of their pants." These are the people who drive by a car lot, see something they like, and before you know it, they have signed on the dotted line. Did they need the new car? Not necessarily. Did they even plan on looking for a new car? The answer is probably not.

Do people who take irresponsible risks have good self-esteem? Possibly they do feel good about themselves in many cases and some are actually successful and productive in our society. But some people take irresponsible risk for outcomes that are substitutes or short-cuts toward a success or goal that they really don't want to work to achieve.

Drug and alcohol abuse are risks some people take everyday for the chance that they will forget their problems or maybe even cause them to go away. In reality those problems only increase. Having a child for the sole purpose of making a bad marriage turn into good is a very dangerous risk and totally irresponsible but occurs far too often.

In summation, the key to taking risks where the chance of success is very probable includes having not only positive self-esteem and confidence, but also being self-actualized to the point where you can develop a strategy that will see the overall worth of the chance being taken.

ARTICLE 52

DOES FEAR
CONTROL YOU?

From our earliest memories we can all remember being scared or afraid at one time or another. Actually there were things that scared us in our infancy that we can't even remember so it's really difficult to determine the first time we were afraid.

Fear is a normal part of living. We all may not remember the first time we were afraid but all of us can most likely remember the last time.

There are certain times the fear makes such an impact in our minds that we will never forget the incident. Some of these moments of fear are family-related and personal, a.k.a. the fear you experience while a loved one is having major surgery or when a child first moves out of the house or goes away to college. Other moments are more generalized in nature.

Being in vehicle accidents or having family members or other loved ones being in danger causes fear of one type. But then there is the fear for everyone's well-being, such as the planes flying into the Twin Towers on 09-01-01. The fear our nation had when Pearl Harbor was bombed or the fear of a local industry closing and your family and the community loosing jobs and trying to face the idea of relocating and re-training.

Some fears are good to have. Strange statement but nevertheless, true. For example, are you afraid to stick your finger in a light socket? Are you afraid to take more medication that is prescribed on the label? Are you afraid to drive faster than the speed limit and risk getting a ticket?

Fear is a critical and positive component of a self-actualized person. Fear is part of maturity. We do not want to do certain things in society for fear of humiliating or hurting our family and friends as well as ourselves.

The problem with fear is when we let it control us. It is not a bad thing to be afraid. It is a bad thing to let the fear control our way of life.

Some people become obsessed with fear due to conditions brought about in their lives that have made such a psychological impact those years of therapy are required to cope. Many times medications are also needed to help ease anxiety for extended periods of time. Probably one of the most traumatic events that result in long-term fear is rape. Other examples include witnessing murders or accidental death, suffering through a devastating fire or being involved in tornadoes, earthquakes or other natural disasters.

Although it is certainly understandable to experience long-term fears, we must cope with these fears if we are going to lead productive lives.

There is nothing to be ashamed about by being afraid. Shame is not a productive solution to conquering fears. Counseling is the best avenue to pursue when fear begins controlling your life. The longer you conduct your life based on avoiding anything that you fear is the longer you will not enjoy a fruitful and productive life.

Working toward self-actualization, with the constant building of self-esteem and goal setting will definitely help defeat fears because in order to move out of your comfort zone and defeat those fears, you have no choice but to control your life and controlling your life means eliminating and controlling your fears and anxieties.

Just for Thought

Don't let fear be your guiding light. But also don't be afraid to take advantage of those resources available to help you with your fight.

Controlling fear is both smart and productive in a self-actualized life. Letting fear control you make you dependent and restrained and allow you no opportunity to move forward.

ARTICLE 53

COOPERATION

All of us have dealt with people who are demanding, uncompromising, and the first individuals we want to avoid anytime we possibly can.

The art of cooperating with others is a necessity for any effective leader. It is also a necessity in moving through life without constant grief and hostility.

Our families are most likely the environment where cooperation is not only needed frequently but can also be the environment where it can become the most volatile. Children fighting over the same toys, teenagers fighting over what television show to watch, and parents fighting over prioritizing which bills to pay, what to buy and how to discipline the kids are all examples each of us has dealt with in our family settings. And cooperation is usually the only way most of these conflicts are settled.

Finding happy mediums in a family situation is difficult to say the least. Trying to find fairness in a home setting is not an easy chore. As parents we try to give everyone a say in our daily routines but many times that fairness idea just doesn't get very far.

To begin with, in order to have cooperation, everyone has to be willing to give up a little. And they have to believe that what the other person is giving up has to be just as important as what they are giving up. If you expect your child to give up watching one television show that is on the same time as another child's favorite show, then that child is going to expect to watch something that is on at the same time his/her sibling has another show on.

I have seen married couples that have saw their marriages end because neither is willing to give up anything, not cooperate with each other on any issue. There are many friendships that have fallen apart because the parties can't cooperate with each other on simple, seemingly ridiculous issues.

Cooperation and team player are almost synonymous. The success of any business is contingent upon cooperation from members of management as well as rank and file. Management teams must arrive at mutually agreed upon goals and objectives to provide a clear picture to staff about what the company is trying to do, how it plans to do it and most importantly, what the employee's roles are in achieving the end result. Employees must cooperate in agreeing to various work rules, salary and fringe benefits, work schedules and grievance procedures. Cooperation from both entities guarantees the opportunity for a win-win situation for the company.

Many companies and industries across this country have closed because of the unwillingness of management and labor to cooperate. No one wins when a company closes. Similarly, in a family situation, no one wins when members can't cooperate with each other. A dysfunctional family is a no win situation for everyone from parents to children.

Any time there is several different personalities wanting the same thing but wanting to achieve it in a different manner, there is going to be discord and stress. Intimidation, demanding threats and just general complaining only lead to unproductive results. Cooperation of all involved is vital for a productive business or personal family life.

So how do you spur cooperation? First it is hard to always be the nucleus of cooperation. It is extremely difficult to be the lone person to try to bring everyone together. Finding a happy medium in a family is most likely as difficult as finding a happy medium on a board of directors. If you find yourself as the individual who is trying to be "peace-maker," remember not to give up all of your needs and desires for you shouldn't find yourself totally unhappy and unfulfilled because that will lead to misery in your own life.

Finally it is important to remember that cooperation is not giving up your ideas and opinions. It is incorporating your ideas and opinions with others to make everyone's ideas and opinions work to the benefit of all. Remember, it takes more self-confidence and a strong self-actualized person to utilize the art of cooperation successfully. Cooperation is a key to success both personally and professionall2y.

ARTICLE 54

HOW WELL DO
YOU LISTEN?

The art of listening has become rare in many parts of our society today. When ask if we are listening we normally will say, "Yes." But are we actually listening or just hearing?

There is a distinct tendency in all of us to only pay attention many times to what is important to us. In other words, if it isn't personal, we tend to let it pass on by. We filter out what we believe is not important to us, what doesn't apply to our current situation, and only absorb what is.

This practice has proven to be dangerous because although the actual subject matter being discussed might not necessarily apply to you at that given moment, what is being said may very well be applicable at a later time and you may have filtered it completely out of you memory.

There are several principles one could use when listening to a speaker but I really think the most important one is: don't talk. Let the person speaking speak! Many people have this innate belief that they cannot be anywhere without making sure everyone knows they are there. Honestly I belief this principle is also simply good manners. Just don't be rude and interrupt or try to talk to someone else while the speaker is saying something.

We need to realize that no matter how hard we try to listen, the chances of us absorbing every tidbit of information is slim. But making a concerted effort to listen will increase your retention rate considerably.

It is true that sometimes we don't always understand the other person's viewpoint. You must approach most conversations with an open mind if you expect to gain any useful information. Just because you may not be agreeing with the speaker's comments and thinking, let the person finish what is being said. After the speaker has finished try to construct your comments in a way that although are not in agreement, are also not offensive. Do not make conversations into arguments. When arguments begin between two people, people fail to listen.

With regard to listening skills involving controversial points of discussion, listen not only to the words but the tone of the speaker. Many times the tone the speaker uses says much more that the words. The loudness of the speaker, whether the voice gets louder or suddenly gets softer, is all indicators as to how the message is being spoken.

One area I have observed with various speakers that confuses many listeners is pausing. Sometimes a speaker will pause for a few moments when talking. Don't give in to the urge to jump in because this is simply the speaker's delivery style. It not only makes you look rude but can also throw off the speaker's line of thinking.

When people talk they are really trying to get their idea across to you. Good listening skills involve being able to put a picture in your mind of what the speaker is saying. If you stay focused on the discussion and avoid distractions you can actually put some type of picture in your mind of the idea the speaker is trying to get across.

Another listening skill is watching for the non-verbal communication. Is the speaker using his/her hands, is there good eye contact with you, and if seated, does the speaker lean toward you or set back? All of these tendencies are part of the speaker communicating the idea to you non-verbally. They are critical in understanding and obtaining information from others.

A final listening skill to mention is preparing you to listen. If you are going into a meeting where what is being said may be critical, try to put as many distractions out of sight and mind as possible. If you are sitting at a desk, clean off the top as much as possible. Don't fight with pencils or papers. Also don't have important conversations in bars or shopping malls where there are a multitude of distractions.

Listening skills are critical to a successful person. They are critical in personal lives as well. How many times has your spouse uttered those famous words, "you don't pay any attention to a damm thing I say?" Well the reality is many times we don't.

We are all guilty of not spending enough time improving our listening skills. I actually believe the older we get the less we really listen. We become "set" in our ways. We don't want to hear about anything we disagree with. It's happening to all of us.

But in this time of a fast-moving society, with internet and cell-phones, and all the technologies that are coming our way daily, it is imperative we listen to what is going on as much as possible. Not just hear, but listen.

ARTICLE 55

COPING WITH
FAILURE

There is none of us that have not failed at something at one point or another in our lives and rest assured we will all fail again at one point or another in the future.

Failure is a part of life. Failure in itself is not necessarily bad. How we cope with failure is much more important than whatever we failed at.

If you make a list of successful people you know or have heard of, one common denominator in every one of them is they failed at one or more times in their quests for success.

So what makes the difference in how you cope with failing? The difference is whether you let that failure affect the rest of your life or do you learn from it and move forward.

Many of us have gone through divorce. Failure of a marriage is usually the result of fault by both parties. Some can rebound with another mate, remarry and have a happy and productive life. There are others who after a divorce, go into a mindset of distrust, bitterness and even hate. These emotions eventually will cause physical health problems such as high blood pressure and heart disease. They will also take you away from socializing with friends and an inability to develop new relationships.

In our work world, failure of a business can result in either the employees moving forward to different and perhaps more rewarding careers or can result in them settling into a mode of being cynical, suspicious, anti social and even lazy. They will make themselves unattractive to potential employers and the intense anger built up within them will eventually cause physical health problems.

There are many ways to define failure. Any time we step outside of our comfort zones we open up the door to potential failure at one point or another. Does that mean we stay within our safety net not trying to improve our lives or do we take the step knowing there will be challenges in our future?

So can we say that failure is in some way a step on the way to success? Is it impossible to be successful in life without experiencing some failures along the way? Most of us don't really remember when we first learned to walk, but I bet we all fell down a lot. When we first tried to ride a bicycle we all wrecked a few times. Great musicians didn't just take a horn or a drum and make great music. These and all other successes, regardless of how huge or how seemingly unimportant, have had their fair share of failing attempts by all of us.

Can we say failure is more mental than physical? In the physical sense the failure is the not achieving of a particular goal. In the mental sense it is the intensity of our belief as to whether we can ever be successful in achieving that particular goal. Sometimes the mental part of failure far exceeds the actual physical failure.

Absolute failure does not occur in most instances unless we give up. With regard to medical situations there are times when a disease or injury has caused a terminal event and obviously the challenge far exceeds the ability to change. When everything has been possibly done to keep a terminal event from occurring and due to circumstances beyond anyone's control dictate the final outcome, there is no failure. The failure is only in not doing everything possible that is available to try to keep that outcome from happening.

With regard to career situations, failure only occurs when we give up on taking advantage of our career opportunities and being complacent with where we are. This is not to say that some people are extremely satisfied with the job they have, the money they make, and the life they lead. The opportunity for failure only occurs when you want to move from one environment to another but don't because you are not comfortable tackling the challenges that may keep you from getting there.

A few things to remember about failure that may help you when you encounter new challenges include remembering that each failure toward a particular goal actually moves you closer to the goal. The more you try to get there the sooner it will happen.

Remember that each time you fail, the fear of failing is going to greatly lessen. Don't look at it as, "you are used to failing." But do look at it as "being used to overcoming challenges." To many people it is not the actual goal they are satisfied with as much as it is overcoming the challenges to get there.

Finally I believe that failures are really not that big a deal if you learn from them and don't let them dictate your life. Failures can make you grow as a person both intellectually and physically. Failures are a part of life they are not your life.

ARTICLE 56

KEEP ON MOVING

There are really only three choices we have in life: (1) Stay Where we are (2) Move Backward (3) Move Forward

Only one of these three choices will ever be synonymous with success. The primary characteristic of the successful person is he or she will find a way to continue to move forward in career and life regardless of the obstacles. What I call a person's "inner drive" will pilot that individual in battling setbacks, going around block aids and searching for new challenges to stimulate and excite as they seek to move forward or it will let that individual be satisfied with whatever life presents and resist any attempt to make a positive change.

I believe moving forward in life is determined by knowing who you are and by knowing where you want to go. I also believe you can't possibly know where you want to go until you know who you are.

When someone asks, "Who are you?", are you honestly ready to answer that question? Usually we respond with our name, maybe our job title or company we work for, but that's pretty much it. Sometimes we may say we are somebody's husband, wife, etc., but that's usually the extent of it.

So try something new and ask yourself who you are. Then really try to answer. Other than your name, age and immediate family members, how much do you really know about yourself? For example: (1) Who do you admire? (2) What makes you mad? (3) Are you spiritual? (4) Is it more important for you to love than to be loved? (5) Do you easily forgive others? (6) Do you easily forgive yourself?

How much do you really know about yourself? Frankly none of us know everything about ourselves. But what we have to do if we want any success at a quality life is continue to learn as much about ourselves as we can.

We don't have someone evaluating our lives and sending us monthly reports. We are tasked with evaluating ourselves on a daily basis and reporting to ourselves. It's called life. When we find parts of our lives we aren't happy with it is up to each of us individually to either change or continue "living with it."

But we need to continually evaluate in order to move in a positive direction. Keep in mind that knowing ourselves has a lot to do with how fast we grow. Knowing who we are determines the people we associate with and finally knowing who we are determines how successful we will be.

Three areas to look at in getting to know yourself are (1) realize how you react to mistakes you make: over react, blame others, accept blame and try to correct; (2) how enthusiastic are you about trying something new: never, not afraid, only when necessary; (3) know your own strengths: positive attitude, love challenges, go along with crowd, passive. I believe if you use these three general evaluative tools it is possible to begin opening the book on knowing yourself.

When people don't know themselves they are unsure of what they want; they don't know what path to take because they don't know where they want to go. Therefore it is impossible to move forward. Complacency or regression is all that can result.

Finally let me point out that complacency is the first step toward regression. Being satisfied with no desire to move forward is the beginning of the end. How many people do you know who are satisfied to live "pay check to pay check," "month-to-month," with no desire to change or even attempt to? Many of these folks also develop the "poor pitiful me" attitude, jealous of others and blaming others for their own misgivings instead of wanting to evaluate their lives, find areas they can change and then putting in the effort and sacrifice to change.

Keep on moving is the key to successful living. If you are unhappy there are reasons. If you are not satisfied with how your life or career is going part of the answer may be you. Remember, we can stay where we are, regress and move backward, or accept the challenges and be willing to take on the sacrifices and determine the path we want in life.

ARTICLE 57

<hr>

WHAT QUESTIONS SHOULD YOU ASK YOURSELF?

Rudyard Kipling one time wrote, "I had six honest serving men, they taught me all I knew: There names were Where and What, When and Why, and How and Who."

There is nothing wrong with being inquisitive but sometimes I wonder if we are inquisitive enough about ourselves. I've talked in various different forums about how important it is to know ourselves before we can possibly know anyone else.

I can tell you I am someone who takes questioning himself to extremes. I tend to double-check and even triple-check my answers to most of the questions I ask myself, whether they be about business, family, church or myself in general. Possibly this started back in my coaching days because during a game the coach must question himself on whether he just made the right strategic decision and then within seconds have to question himself about what is the best decision for the next play. After completing an approximately 40-year coaching career I have come to realize that "questioning practice" has actually became a part of my life.

What I have tried to do rather than "trash" the way I question myself is to move my process of questioning what I do into my current lifestyle. Now sometimes I can tell you it drives my family and friends crazy. "Why do you keep second-guessing yourself?", I hear over and over. Well for one, old habits are hard to break. But more importantly as I have questioned myself over the years, I have learned a lot about myself. And I have come to the realization that I really don't know myself nearly as well as I thought I did nor as well as I should.

Getting to know you better is the absolute best reason anyone should ask his or her self questions. Keep in mind that there is one major pre-requisite for asking yourself questions: you must answer yourself honestly. Lying to yourself may make you feel good temporarily but it won't help you in the long-term.

You can most likely classify all the questions you may ever ask yourself into one of three categories: (1) Open-door questions (2) Closed-Door questions or (3) the Yes or No question.

Open-door questions are those which use the who, what, where, when, how and why words. When you question yourself in this manner you are giving yourself a lot of room to expand your thoughts. That is a good thing. You question yourself about who is involved with you in a particular scenario, what is going on, when will it happen and how difficult or easy it will be to accomplish something. Of course the why is always hard because you then have to evaluate if whether what you are doing is worth the result. Do the positives outweigh the negatives?

We ask ourselves closed-door questions when we want to clarify or emphasize just how much we want something to happen or not. Asking yourself, "Just exactly what do I know about this?", "What consequences do I see happening if I do this?", or "What is going to be the hardest part of this for me?", are examples of questions designed to really start pinning yourself down on the task at hand.

The Yes or No question is simple and bottom line: a direct response. "Do I know exactly why I need to do this?", "Am I prepared to accept the consequences of what I am either doing or about to do?", "Is this decision one that will improve my future?, all questions with a yes or no answer. This is direct and to the point.

I have found that not just in coaching but in almost all aspects of my life, this is the basic plan for making decisions. It requires knowing me. And with some of these questions, if I am not happy with the honest answer I give myself, I go back and look at why I answered the way I did.

Asking yourself questions, providing you are answering truthfully, is a great measuring stick on how well you know yourself. And of course its always possible based on our answers, that we really don't like the person we are questioning. We just don't like the person we are. Next is the big challenge: making the changes necessary. Questioning ourselves and answering ourselves honestly is like looking in the mirror: the refection doesn't lie.

ARTICLE 58

STRATEGIES
FOR COPING

Several years ago in one of my leadership classes there was a discussion about coping with the pressures of business which I think also applies to life in general: "Set your standards high, try to do the absolute best you are capable of doing and focus on running the race rather than winning it. Do those things necessary to bring out your personal best and don't loose sleep worrying about the competition. Let the competition loose sleep worrying about you."

Shouldn't that advice be applied to our everyday lives? Coping with the daily rigors of life can be intense and can affect your relationships with family and friends, career, health and the desire to even get out of bed each day.

The most important key in my opinion to successfully coping with the problems of life is to begin by realizing you are NOT the "bad guy." Blaming you for everything and being the "martyr" is the absolute worst way to cope with any issue.

There are a million different theories about how to cope. Which one works for you is obviously the one you need to use? I want to discuss four I think are of primary use in most everyday situations:

(1) Managing yourself and your time. If you are disorganized you are not going to be able to cope with any situation. You must make an attempt, at the minimum, to organize your day. Either the night before or even in the morning before you start your day, put some type of organization into how you are going to move forward. Your own disorganization causes everyone around you to be disorganized. Not getting your kids out of bed to go to school on time, not getting them breakfast before they go to school, not washing their clothes (or yours) the night before and even not getting to work on time are just some very basic ways to have chaos and unnecessary stress even before you leave the house.

(2) Don't practice avoidance. One thing I have learned over the years is that any time I put off dealing with a problem it is only going to come back to "bite me" again harder and at a more inconvenient time than the present. Force yourself to deal with the problem of the moment immediately, or a least begin to deal with it. For sure some problems take longer to solve than others. But the initial attempt at working the problem out at least means you recognize the issue for what it is and realize the potential consequences of avoiding.

(3) Keep things in perspective. I have always believed the saying, "don't strangle on an ant and swallow an elephant." What this means is we need to realize what problems are and which ones are only day to day issues that will take care of themselves. Some people have the desire to jump on things they really have no control over, i.e. the weather, a water line break, heavy traffic going to or from work. Etc. These are things that inconvenience all of us at one time or another but we have to make up our minds to just deal with them and move forward. We can't control the weather but if it looks like rain, take an umbrella. We can't control how old the water lines are in our town but one is going to break sooner or later, just realize the city will fix it because you for certain are not going to. And if you know traffic is going to be heavy going to work in the mornings, just leave earlier. Complaining about those things takes your mind off the big issues, things you can make a difference with.

(4) Find time to relax. This one goes back to organization and managing your time. Chaos has no time to rest. It starts, grows and grows and then explodes. The key to controlling and eliminating chaos is getting organized. Control that which you can control and save the time and energy necessary to handle the big problems. So organize your day and set aside an hour or so for yourself. Take a walk, take a nap, just sit and listen to music or watch the cars go by. Relaxing is a great coping mechanism.

Its important to remember that coping is a process that has been going on since the beginning of time. Pioneers coped with the elements. Certain animal species cope with surviving every day with other species that are trying to eat them. Our ancestors coped with cold weather and little heat, hot weather and no air conditioning. And we all cope with loosing loved ones, loosing jobs, loosing marriages. Its all about how we face it, the attitude we have, developing our priorities. Its all about setting our standards high, facing our problems head on and doing the absolute best we are capable of doing to bring out our personal best.

AFTERWORD

DAYMAR COMMENCEMENT SPEECH - Saturday, August 6, 2011 - 2PM

On August 6, 2011, I had the honor of being the commencement speaker at Daymar College's graduation. Where these graduates are today I have no way of knowing but I do know they knew how to succeed in class and I truly believe many are very successful in their chosen careers. I wanted to add the speech to this book to illustrate the results of high self-esteem, self-worth and a fantastic desire for personal growth.

First my thanks to Daymar College, Rebecca Mowry and everyone for asking me to be here. It is quite an honor to speak to you this afternoon.

And it truly is an honor to be standing here in front of this wonderful group of graduates. You people represent what is really important in our country. You have proven, many times through personal hardship and sacrifice, that true success can be attained if you persevere.

I really don't have any idea what each of you sacrificed to make it to this point in your lives, but I know it wasn't all an easy journey.

Some of you came to Daymar right out of high school. Unsure about the future, maybe even a little scared. You left the security of a very structured high school routine and came into a situation where school buses don't pick you up, mom might not wake you up in the morning, and when Friday nights were for ballgames and parties. All this replaced with going to class, finding a job and suddenly not even seeing your high school buddies

147

because many of them suddenly didn't have any more time for you than you did for them. But you know what? You overcame, you made it! You are here!

Some of you came to Daymar while raising a family. Some of you are single-parents. You got up early in the morning. You got your kids ready for school, got them on the bus, maybe even took them to school. And then maybe drove like crazy to get to class on time. And there were times when you needed a babysitter at the last minute because the regular one cancelled out. And you couldn't come to school so you called, got your assignment, watched your kids and got the work done. There were times when in the middle of the night, after you had been up studying all night, you kid wakes up with an upset stomach, fever, whatever, and you call ER, maybe even take the kid over to the hospital, get no sleep and then suddenly its time to go to class. Maybe you end up missing the class or show up and sit there is a daze. It happens. You miss seeing your kid play a little league game, a school play, because you only have so much time to study. But you know what? You overcame, you made it! You are here!

And then there are some of you who decided after the kids were raised, maybe a spouse has passed away or you just want to prove something to yourself, came to Daymar. You were out of school for a long time, you raised a family, did the PTA thing, worked with girl scouts, little league, and now the kids are gone and you refuse sit alone. Nervous? Certainly. Scared? Sure. You found life outside of the family-atmosphere possibly even shocking. You worked hard...you studied hard, you worried that your age, time away from school, and maybe even the *discouragement* of some of your "friends," were all reasons to quit. To give it up. But you know what? You overcame, you made it! You are here!

Whether some of you fit into any of these scenarios or not I have no way of really knowing. But I do know the road to where you are today was challenging, both personally and with your classes. I congratulate you all. I tell you I am so very proud and honored to be here with you.

To your families, I ask you to give these people a hug, shake their hand, love them, respect them and always admire them.

Thank you.

Printed in the United States
By Bookmasters